Leslie Linsley's
15 - MINUTE
Decorating Ideas

BOOKS BY LESLIE LINSLEY

Leslie Linsley's
15-MINUTE
Decorating Ideas

LESLIE LINSLEY
Illustrations by Jon Aron

ST. MARTIN'S GRIFFIN
New York

Designed by Bonni Leon-Berman

ISBN 0–312–14117–3

First St. Martin's Griffin Edition: April 1996

Contents

Introduction

When I was growing up, my mother and I would go shopping in the fanciest home-furnishings boutiques and department stores in New York City. Mostly we were attracted to the one-of-a-kind handmade items. But we never bought anything we saw because every time one of us liked something my mother would say, "We don't have to buy it. We'll make it ourselves." Some of the things we did make, but many times we forgot about it as soon as we got home. Later, having come from a fairly handy family, I did make things for my own home and learned quite a few crafts. Little did I know when I was a small child that I would end up making a career of writing about how to create your own style on less money and without spending lots of time doing it.

Decorators, artists, and designers have always come up with innovative ideas for interior decoration. The difference between them and the rest of the world is that they have the confidence to improvise. The most creative and interesting rooms are those in which the owners have a flair for using everyday objects in unexpected ways. Style has little to do with money. The most interesting rooms are those furnished with an eclectic mix of objects. It's just a matter of looking at things in a fresh way and putting them together imaginatively. And since most of us have limited time it's always fun to learn new ways to achieve a designer look without making a career out of it.

Cheap chic seems to be "in." Shopping at discount stores, mixing unfinished furniture with antiques, adding newly purchased collectibles with early folk art, and finding clever alternatives to solving decorating problems that might otherwise be costly is what I like to do best. Furnishing a house has gotten very expensive, especially if you're starting from scratch. There are so many beautiful accessories on the market, like pillows, in gorgeous fabrics— all tablecloths and curtains—as well as all the other things that make a room special. Rather than not having them because of a budget that doesn't stretch beyond the basics, find out how to have it all for less, and how to do it in just fifteen minutes, here and there.

I've been writing about decorating, crafts, and how to create your own style for a long time. I'm always on the lookout for new materials and new ways to do things. Beyond decorating, there is general maintenance of the materials in a home and fix-up techniques that you might not be aware of. Many manufacturers have supplied me with information that will help in all areas of home style and, where possible, I've included consumer hotlines for you to use to obtain more and specific information. The book is laid out in a quick-read format so you can find everything—from what color to paint your walls to how to slipcover an ottoman—in seconds.

Writing a weekly newspaper column called, "Home Style" and owning a store in a resort area, have contributed greatly to my awareness of what people are doing in their own homes, how they are solving problems, and what products are available to decorating-conscious do-it-yourselfers. Whether you're furnishing your very first home, whether you live in a city townhouse or a country cottage, whether you're decorating an entire house or just want an innovative way to tie back your living room drapes, you'll find it here in a no-nonsense approach that takes the mystique out of decorating and makes it fun.

The Basics

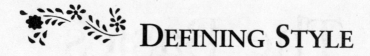 # DEFINING STYLE

Everyone has likes and dislikes in all areas. When it comes to decorating it's easier than you might think to define your style. And it's important to do this before purchasing expensive items such as sofas and wall units.

Color

Color is very subjective. Most people are quite definite about the colors they like and don't like. This is a good place to start when defining your style. Make a list of the colors that please you and those that don't. Then imagine living with these colors in every room of the house.

How Do You Live?

Do you feel best when you're surrounded by comfortable things? Do you like a formal environment? Do you like to eat most meals in the kitchen, or do you prefer eating dinner in a dining room? How do you entertain? These are some of the questions to answer in order to define your style.

Areas of the Country Influence Style

Regional decorating doesn't have to reflect where you live, although it usually does. In the Southwest, for example, you might choose desert colors and Santa Fe–style furniture. If you live in New England you might be more inclined to choose country-style furnishings. Bright colors are more appropriate in tropical areas than in northern climates. Chances are you'll be influenced by what you see around you, but if you like a style from another region, introduce some of these ideas within your own regional style.

Country Versus Contemporary

The type of home you live in will influence your style. If it's a country home, your style of furniture might be warm woods and accessories such as quilts, pottery, folk art, and other handmade items. If you live in a city apartment or townhouse your style might lean toward contemporary, and appropriate furnishings would be glass and chrome or formal woods. This is not to say that a country theme would be out of place in a city dwelling. In fact, this can be a nice way to warm up a contemporary environment. But deciding what you like is how you define your style.

Trying Out Different Styles

It's a good idea to get as much information as possible before you begin any decorating project. Look through the decorating magazines. Take a tour of a decorator showhouse if there is one in your area. Often local garden clubs hold regular tours through people's homes. Check this out. It's lots of fun and you can get all sorts of good ideas. Look through the style books. There's one on every subject imaginable. Study set-up rooms in the furniture section of department stores. You will very quickly realize what you like and don't like and this will help define your style.

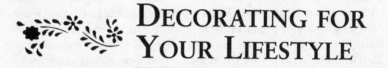

DECORATING FOR YOUR LIFESTYLE

Everyone is lightening up on decorating: using less-heavy fabric to cover windows; removing unnecessary knickknacks; simplifying patterns, colors, and accessories. We are all trying to make our homes look good without becoming a slave to them.

Comfort First

When decorating a room think about how it will be used. Go through your routine. Ask yourself basic questions such as: Do I entertain often? How do I entertain—for dinner, brunch, cocktails, cookouts? How many people do I enjoy having over at a given time? Where does the family like to gather? How does the room accommodate our leisure activities?

Furnish the room to make it work by putting comfort first. Pretty fabrics can be practical. Just because a room is comfortable doesn't mean it has to be shabby. Slipcovers are a good decorating solution in homes where there are children.

Yard Sale and Flea Market Finds

It doesn't have to cost a fortune to be a decorating find. In fact the most interesting pieces I've ever seen came from foraging. The owners knew how to spot items with good potential and made the most of it. The things you find and sometimes makeover are often the very things that make a room sing.

Great Cover-Ups

New paint, paper, and fabric can brighten up or modernize. Paint old dark wood with white enamel. Add bright, pretty floral-chintz fabric to dining room seats and use unfinished furniture pieces for decorative paint techniques. Sand an old wood floor and give it a paint treatment such as a checkerboard pattern. Create a wall of built-in cabinets with unfinished ones placed side by side. Then use one of the all-in-one varnish/wood stains in the color of your choice.

QUESTIONS FOR A DECORATOR

If the thought of decorating an entire house—or even one room—is overwhelming, you might consider hiring a design consultant. In fact, many home-furnishing stores have an in-house designer, or the owner might be an interior designer. Some places don't charge for consulting if you buy your furnishings from them. However, there are many good professional interior designers who can help you plan your home within your budget and, in most cases, will be able to buy through design showrooms at discount prices. Here are some questions to ask that might help.

1. What is the fee for the first consultation? It is important to see if you and the designer can work well together.
2. How do they charge? By the hour? By the room? Is there one set fee for the project?
3. Don't be intimidated if you want to redecorate only a small part of the house at a time. Ask if they can help you make a master plan that may never go beyond one room, or if they can make a plan that you can implement yourself over a period of time.
4. If you buy something on your own, or already have things you want to keep, is this a problem? (If you consult a decorator in a department store, ask if you have to buy everything from that store alone.)
5. Can you make some of your old things work by reupholster-

ing or slipcovering them? (Whenever possible try to recycle if saving money is a major consideration.).

6. If you make a plan for the entire project, does the decorator have a problem if you don't do everything at once? (If so, she or he isn't right for you.)

7. Present a budget and define what you want to accomplish within it. Is this a problem? If so, what would be the recommendation?

8. Tell the decorator about your lifestyle and how you want to use each room. Tell him or her your favorite colors and ask if they seem appropriate for what's currently the style in fabrics, etc.

9. Be open minded about new ideas that might not be what you originally had in mind. Take the opportunity to be exposed to new things, but also be definite about what you don't like. You should never be stuck with something you know in your heart of hearts you can't live with.

10. Don't ever let the decorator come between you and your partner. For example, if you and your decorator love a certain fabric, but your spouse hates it, find another fabric. It's not worth fighting about.

11. If this isn't the house you plan to live in forever, let the decorator know so you can select wisely. In other words, you might not want to put lots of money into window treatments that may not fit your next home. But you might want to purchase a good sofa and chairs with timeless fabric that will work anywhere.

12. Where do you find a decorator? Check out the local Yellow Pages, call the ASID consumer referral hotline (800–775–ASID), ask at your local home-furnishings store (many have in-store design consultants and don't charge for this service), visit model homes in the area, or get references from neighbors.

 # AT HOME

 I love being home. I love making my home satisfy my aesthetic and emotional needs. I love making it function for what I'm doing at different times. I mostly love it when it's neat. I don't always work better in a neat environment, but my emotional stability level is higher. When I'm working at peak I like a certain amount of messiness. When things are too neat I tend not to want to start a project, because I know the path it takes. First the material is laid out and kept in check, but as I get more involved things get more out of hand, until they go beyond the point of reasonable sanity. Then it takes planning a party, going away, or something catastrophic to move me to get back to go.

But I love my home. I don't find anything more compelling going on outside of my little sphere to draw me away. If your home isn't the place you'd most like it to be, perhaps you can make it so. Many people I talk to say they get cabin fever if they're home for too long. On the weekend they try to plan events and activities that take them away from their homes. Here are some ways to change all that:

1. Take up an indoor hobby such as craft and create a place to do it. Then outfit that space with everything you need to do this craft efficiently. If you like to sew, for example, make a sewing area that's just perfect for your projects. Or take up quilting. Not only is this the perfect craft to relax you after work, but also you will be making something to enhance your home.

2. Find a sunny window and create a nesting spot. You might place a small table and comfortable chair here so that you can sit and read, have a cup of coffee, or just gaze out the window.

3. Attach a bird feeder to your window. You'll be amazed at how fascinating birdwatching can be.
4. Grow seeds in a window box indoors. Arrange plants both large and small, and perfect your indoor garden.
5. Arrange your furniture for optimum use. Make one area for entertaining, another for relaxing.
6. Have short-term and long-term in-house projects going on at all times. In this way you can quilt, for example, for an hour or two. When you get tired of that you might work at your computer for awhile, and then rearrange your sweater drawer.
7. Plan to cook all day Sunday once a month. You can stock your freezer with meals. But plan ahead so you have all the ingredients. I can't tell you how wonderful it is to come home to a meal I cooked a month ago. It's like going to someone else's house for dinner.
8. Correspondence is something we all let slide. But if you have a well-stocked desk with greeting cards, pretty stationery, and a sheet of stamps along with nice pens that feel good to use, you'll be drawn to keeping in touch. Then it isn't a chore, but rather a wonderful distraction.
9. Keep up with your photo albums. I tend to throw all my snapshots into one drawer or a shoebox. Every now and then I take out the scissors and tape and choose the best ones for the album. Having the supplies at hand makes this a lot easier when you get the urge to do it. So get the extra pages and plan to do this one afternoon while sitting at your sunny window.
10. If the house needs attention with a major spruce-up like a paint job, plan to do one area at a time and make this a long-term project. Even these fix-ups that we tend to put off can be extremely satisfying. Every hour you put into improving your home is like money in the bank.
11. If you never have time to read, make the time on weekends. Buy the books you're attracted to when you find them, even if you don't have the time right away to read them. Stack the books on a chair or small table so you can take your pick depending on your mood. If they're in front of you all the time, eventually you may feel like reading rather than going out.

12. If possible, food shop during the week so you'll have the things you love in the house on the weekend, just in case you'd rather stay home than do anything else.

RELAXED STYLE

An overwhelming interest in flea market, antique, and yard sale decorating has been sweeping the country. Many of us are tired of being told how to have a perfectly beautiful home. It takes effort. It's hard to live a normal life and keep a house looking like the pages of a magazine at all times. So it isn't surprising that so many people are embracing the idea of "cheap chic" or eclectic style. It's just more comfortable to create a combination of things you find and love. It's more practical to have a coffee table on which you can rest your feet than a coffee table reserved only for a gorgeous vase filled with fresh flowers and a few ceramics placed at just the right angle.

Family Style

Most environments inhabited by real families eventually become relaxed. Things creep into our rooms that make it hard to maintain a stylish look. There are books, magazines, and newspapers on chairs and tables. A china cabinet might be brimming with too many uninteresting things, obliterating the carefully arranged chinaware. Give yourself permission to let things get out of hand from time to time. If you don't let it go on too long you can make a clean sweep from time to time. In this way you won't drive yourself crazy with the impossible task of keeping things pristine all the time.

A Page Out of a Decorating Magazine

Few of us can live on a magazine set. But we like it when things are pretty. It gives us pleasure to walk through rooms that are well designed, where furniture is carefully placed. So what are we to do? Rearranging furniture from time to time gives a room a lift. It will seem less tired even if you can't afford to buy new things. Adding a vase of fresh cut flowers will do wonders, and putting away all knickknacks will also help give a room a new look. Then carefully add one item at a time. Live with it before adding another.

Spare Is Special

Spare, monochromatic rooms don't necessarily have to look bare. Natural colors make a room look fresh and up-to-date, and the absence of excess can be quite sophisticated. Start with natural-colored canvas, sailcloth, or linen slipcovers. Add a few occasional pillows made from vintage fabrics to your sofa, a soft mohair throw over a chair, and exchange your old coffee table for a garden table made of teak or wrought iron and you'll instantly have a new look. Fill a basket with pots of violets for a splash of color and your house will look sensational with very little effort.

DECORATING TRENDS: WHERE DO THEY COME FROM?

A couple of years ago Sister Parish died. For those who may not know, she was the grande dame of American interior decorating. Her six decades in the decorating business started in 1933 in one room in New Jersey and evolved into the noted decorating firm of Parish-Hadley Associates, based in Manhattan. Their designs consistently exuded quality. Her style was a homey, traditional, undecorated look—charm without gimmickry. "What seems important to me," she was quoted as saying, "is permanence, comfort, and a look of continuity in the design and decoration of a house." She is associated with beautiful, familiar things, and the firm, noted for the handsomeness of their work, is affordable only to a well-heeled clientele. She redecorated the Kennedy White House as well as the homes of her most discerning friends.

Country Style

The concept of decorating is relatively new to the majority of people in this country. While Americans have always been fascinated with the British style of decorating, it was enjoyed only by the wealthy who could afford a professional to "do" their homes. But that was before "country style."

Sister Parish defined the first version of American Country without naming it anything but "traditional." She decorated with patchwork quilts, four-poster beds, painted floors, and rag rugs, which at the time, seemed innovative rather than old-fashioned. She prided herself on being able to reach into the past in order to bring back what she knew to be "good, beautiful, and lasting."

Country Style Revisited

Not until a generation later, when Mary Emmerling, an editor at *House Beautiful,* introduced us to a version of this style, did it became accessible to more than just a handful of wealthy clients. Emmerling put together rooms and gave them a label. And finally, manufacturers brought us products so that anyone could afford to create "American Country" style.

Americans flocked to a trend created with the very things that were right under our noses. But it didn't happen overnight. Unlike a passing fad, this particular style of decorating crept into our collective consciousness slowly, over a period of ten years, before it was finally declared a bona fide trend. And then we were bombarded with everything that looked like it had been in our grandmothers' attics all along, just waiting to be discovered. In other words, everyone found that somewhere in their home—or garage—was an item with decorative potential. Unlike traditional or contemporary, country style caught on because it had the right combination of elements. It was livable, recognizable, accessible, and affordable.

Creating a Style

Style has a way of repeating itself in all arenas. The cycles go on, with variations on each theme, making trends both familiar and new at the same time. We're comfortable with change only when there is the essence of something known. If the familiar element is too recent, the style seems stale, overused. But if it simply has the faintest sense of the familiar, we embrace it as new.

Something Old Is New

It's been a long time since anything fresh and new was introduced to take the place of country style, but the desire is there because early American country has been overdone and it's a little tired. In the last year or two a style has begun to emerge in the form of furnishings that look interesting because—surprise! surprise!—the rooms are put together with yard sale, auction, flea market, antique, and bargain finds. Besides being livable and affordable, this trend has the magic ingredient of *looking* new even though it's made up of old or recycled things. It's exciting. And anyone can pull it off with a little help from the stylemakers who are showing them how it's done. It's an easy trend to build upon because everything has possibilities and there are unusual items everywhere in the country. Best of all, this type of decorating evolved from what has become an interesting and inexpensive leisure activity. Everyone enjoys the hunt!

Eclectic Style

The designer Robert Venturi and his wife introduced the original concept of eclectic decorating—designing interiors by combining styles and furniture from all over the world. The popular version might be defined as "yard-sale chic." It's okay to put a Chippendale in the same room with a humble, painted kitchen table. Eclectic is not one thing. It's variety and it's hard to label with any word that explains it other than "antistyle."

Putting It Together

Like new trends in fashion, presentation is everything. When *Vogue* magazine shows models dressed in ripped jeans or clothes from Army Navy Stores, they pair the clothing with shoes from designers like Susan Bennis and Warren Edwards and gold earrings from the Paloma Picasso Collection. Without this combination of high-end and low-end items, the entire "look" doesn't succeed.

"Yard-sale chic" is the right combination of junk and jewels. If this trend goes the way decorators, manufacturers, magazine editors, and designers are predicting, it will replace American country and will be with us for a long, long time.

REGIONAL INFLUENCES

I love visiting other parts of the country and bringing home ideas to use in my own region. It might be a color of paint or a small detail such as shuttered window treatments. As a Northerner I particularly enjoyed my first trip to Charleston, South Carolina. The similarities I found between Southern houses and New England homes was most interesting. This doesn't seem so unusual since the oldest homes in the country are found along the eastern seacoast. But I was expecting to see "Tara" on every street. Yes, there are reminders everywhere of *Gone with the Wind*, with names like Rhett house or street, and of course there's the Ashley and Cooper rivers that shape the peninsula on which the city is built, but more homes are modest than the stately antebellum homes we associate with this area.

Historic Influences

Preservation is uppermost in this three-hundred-year-old city, renowned for its splendid architecture. Charleston's historic district encompasses more than two-thousand historic buildings; seventy-three predate the Revolutionary War; 136 are from the late 1700s; and more than six-hundred others were built in the early 1800s. Two of the most prominent features of the historic district are the major architectural styles; the double house and the single house. The front doors of the double house face the street, with one room to either side. The typical single house is only one room wide with the narrow gable end turned toward the street. To one side is a door that opens onto a piazza, this city's version of a veranda or what we in the north call a porch. I think "piazza" sounds so much nicer and maybe we should think about renaming our plain porches, piazzas. The main entrances face the side, reached by way of a courtyard or through an ornate wrought-iron gateway. This, I was told, is because taxes were levied according to how many feet of a house faced the street. Similar houses were built during the eighteenth and nineteenth centuries in New Orleans for this reason.

Shutters Are Practical

Many of Charleston's homes are made of brick and most houses have solid shutters on the first floor windows and louvered shutters on the upstairs windows. I imagine that residents, because they live so close to the street, must keep the windows shuttered for privacy and noise control. In Key West, Florida, louvered Bahamian shutters cover the entire windows on the facade of a house and open outward from the bottom to allow air circulation while keeping the effects of the blazing sun at bay. They are often painted a contrasting color such as green or aqua. They are practical and good looking.

Paint Colors

We often find that paint colors used on houses and interiors are different in different parts of the country. A common sight in Charleston is the color green. Just as in New England we find lots of Colonial gray, barn red, and Newport blue, Charleston has a green that is seen on everything from shutters to front doors to piazza trim. It is a dark hunter color made by mixing a little pigment of yellow with black. In recent years the desert colors of Santa Fe have had a big influence on the rest of the country.

Gardens

Charleston residents are most proud of their gardens, and everything in them seems to spring to life at once. Even the most unimposing homes have courtyard gardens, but to see the really grandest of plantation gardens one has only to pick from a vast array of public gardens in and around the city. Magnolia Plantation and Gardens on the Ashley River is a five-hundred-acre estate acquired in 1676 by the Drayton family whose heirs still own it. The fifty-acre garden, begun a decade later, now contains nine-hundred varieties of camellias, 250 types of azaleas, and hundreds of other flowering species. The manor house depicts plantation living since the Civil War. And this is only one of many to see.

Local Crafts

When visiting other parts of the country we often find local crafts that we don't find at home. In Charleston, one sees women sitting on street corners making hay straw baskets and hats. It's always fun to find something to decorate your home as a reminder of the area.

Putting It All Together

The point I'm trying to make is that you can develop new decorating ideas simply by keeping attuned to how other people have solved problems similar to yours. Whenever you travel, be aware of color combinations used in homes, on shopfronts, and even on local signs. Notice how windows, porches, and walkways are handled, and how different neighborhoods make use of flowers and planters. Watch for local crafts and customs. Remember what you like and try to incorporate these new treatments into your own eclectic look.

Colors

Choosing a Color

When faced with bare walls or a bare room, choosing the right colors can be daunting. Color is the beginning of good design and a way to express the mood you want to create. Some rooms are better left white; others look best when filled with a riot of color.

Old-Fashioned Advice for What It's Worth

I recently went to a yard sale and couldn't resist a book called *How to Be Your Own Decorator* written in 1926 by the director of *Good Housekeeping* Studio. So popular was it back then that it had three reprintings. I discovered that things haven't changed much since the early 1920s, to judge by this statement: "Today there is an increasing appreciation of color and knowledge of how to use it." But then they go on with this silly advice, "No color scheme can be really successful that does not use three or more colors."

Black and White Is Always Classic

A basic black-and-white color scheme can be bold and crisp and is always exciting. There are many ways to use a black-and-white theme effectively, adding color sparingly when desired.

- Black-and-white ticking is great for slipcovers because it's sturdy, inexpensive, and good looking. Use yellow floral throw pillows with it for summer and change to bright red in the winter for an easy change of decor. Slipcovers made from ticking can be easily washed and will get softer and better looking with wear. Try using the reverse side of the fabric for a toned-down gray-and-white stripe.

- Slipcovers for the living room can be made from off-white canvas or sailcloth, washable linen, or heavy cotton. Cover cording with black fabric for the piping and combine black and white fabrics for throw pillows.

- If you have a center hallway or family room, a black-and-white tile floor is practical and good looking. It's also easy to care for. The trick to making it look interesting is to set twelve-inch squares on the diagonal, giving you a diamond grid. For a bathroom, combine four-inch white ceramic tile with two-inch black tiles.

- Inexpensive but handsome café curtains can be made for the kitchen or bathroom from black-and-white plaid dishtowels. Best of all there's no sewing involved. Attach evenly spaced clip-on curtain rings to the top edge of each towel and hang on a rod.

- For a dramatic window treatment, buy plain white, inexpensive draperies and trim the edge with black grosgrain ribbon or a band of black printed fabric. Then add matching tiebacks for a custom-made look.

- After you've combined the black and white for a bold contrasting color scheme, add one bright color for accent. It might be yellow or red in small accessories that can be changed when desired. You might add color in the form of plants or vases to hold cut flowers. Or, introduce a small, painted occasional table. If you have a sideboard or china cabinet with glass doors, add colorful dishes. Frame pictures in black or white frames.

Adding Warmth to Black and White

If you think the black-and-white color scheme is too stark, especially for winter coziness, it's easy to combine warm natural colors in the form of pillows, a tablecloth, bedspread, soft mohair throw, and baskets. Use the warm-colored accessories now, then remove them in the spring for a fresh, cool environment.

PAINT COLORS

Every season brings with it a new palette of "hot" colors. If pastels are in this year, they are bound to be out the next. Recently I was advising a couple about paint colors for their newly built first home. At first they wanted the entire house to be all white. There's something about a brand new home that makes us reluctant to mess it up with color. But then they visited a home in which each room was a different color. The effect was so stunning that it changed their thinking, and now they wanted to know what colors should be used where.

Balancing Act

We use color to achieve a level of comfort, visually and physically, in our spaces. A balance of color is the goal. Jarring changes of ill-matched colors from room to room create chaos. Color sets a mood and helps develop a room's character. Always use the colors that please you most. And when choosing a color, think about this in relation to what it is that makes you enjoy being in certain rooms you've known.

Blue Doesn't Bring on the Blues

There are some color schemes that are always in style. Perhaps this is because they are so easy to live with and make a room and the things in it look so good we never tire of them. This is true with blue. A blue-and-white scheme is always refreshing. It is especially popular for the bedroom and always on porches and in vacation homes. Recently, the adored member of the blue family is periwinkle.

Green Is Growing

Green is growing on us as a really interesting paint color, especially in the forest or hunter shades, for such rooms as the den or outdoor porches. Different shades of green such as olive and pine will always be in style. I especially like a pale, pale celery green for a dining room. Couple this with white or off-white trim for an elegant look. Then add old-world tapestry fabric to the dining chair seats for a formal look, or a floral chintz for a summery, more casual environment.

See Red

Cherry, vermilion, cranberry, brick, terra-cotta, cinnamon, barn, and Christmas reds are all easy colors to live with, and they work well with other colors in decorating schemes. They are classic as main colors and useful for accenting a room with accessories such as throw pillows or for painted trim.

Naturally Speaking

Monochromatic shades are restful and easy to live with. With a natural background you can introduce all sorts of different hues and change the look of a room often. Nature's colors have always been foolproof and, when used in interesting combinations, can be anything but boring. Combine putty, coral, different desert tones like sand, and other light and dark shades of natural. For some brightness, coral is punchy and soothing at the same time.

White for Special Occasions

A white background is the only one worth using if you have wonderful elements such as paintings, collections, furniture, and fabrics. White ties the elements together and helps them to relate to each other. White also comes in an endless variety of shades, allowing you to create a lively or serene environment.

Black and White

A classic, bold combination, this one will never be dated. You will see black-and-white painted checkerboard floors, for example, in early Federal homes, sleek contemporary houses, and country cottages. A black-and-white color scheme has and probably always will be associated with contemporary rooms. You can add any vivid color such as magenta, sunflower, teal, or more subdued colors to this background.

Painted Techniques

A decorative painted treatment such as ragging, sponging, or marbling can transform walls and give a room character. If you've

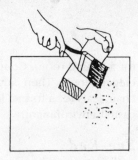

never done this before and would like to try, start with a small room such as a bathroom, or one wall, perhaps behind the bed. Painting techniques are acquired and one tends to get better with practice.

One Color Throughout

A small house benefits from the use of one color throughout. This creates a balanced flow and makes the space seem larger. To create a cozy feeling in a small space, dark colors often work best. Or, for a light feeling, use creamy colored paint for the walls and a very light pastel shade of color, such as aqua, for the ceiling.

Accent the Accents

Heavy wood molding always makes a room more interesting. Paint the ceiling and walls eggshell and treat the molding with a wood stain or paint it a shade of gray or beige. Shutters on windows can be treated in the same way as the molding.

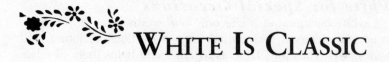

WHITE IS CLASSIC

When it comes to decorating, you can never go wrong with white. It is the perfect color and noncolor for a background into which color can be introduced. With white you can mix all sorts of different accessories and they won't clash. White lightens and brightens any room. It's safe while being daring at the same time. White expresses many moods. When everything in a room is white or natural, the overall effect can be immediately inviting, cool, elegant, and soothing.

White never seems to go out of style. If you buy something you love in white, it will dictate many more such purchases. In fact, you may find it so appealing you'll want to add color carefully.

Starting with Paint

Young couples often ask me where to start when decorating a first home. You will never get sick of white. Once you've got your basic pieces and have painted the walls, you can add color wherever you want it. But if you start with a color on the walls you have to design around it, and if you use a particularly bright color you can get mighty tired of it after a few months.

What Shade of White?

There are, of course, many shades of white—from hospital white to linen and eggshell to pearl to rose petal and beyond. But if white is too bland for your taste consider a faux finish for texture. You just paint on the base coat, let it dry, and then sponge, comb, rag, or stipple a glaze coat in the same color or a contrasting shade. Formby's Decorative Touches line of products has come out with the glaze mix in a kit that makes this amazingly simple to do. You just mix the glaze (which comes in dark, light, and clear) with your background paint and apply it in your chosen pattern. It takes the guesswork out of mixing just the right shade of glaze and it washes up with water.

Au Naturel

An ideal combination: White with natural wood, muted Indian rugs with bare wooden floor showing all around, throw pillows made from soft vintage fabrics, woven throws tucked over seat cushions, and all-white tulips in clear glass vases.

Quick-Change Artist

When your furniture is covered with white canvas or sailcloth it's easy to warm it up or cool it down for the change of seasons. Use different tones of brown and earth tones with a basic white scheme for a sophisticated look that's always in style.

Isn't White Impractical?

Unfortunately, most people think white is impractical. A friend once rented a summer vacation house that was all white and bright except for the furniture. The sofas and chairs were upholstered with brown tweed and it ruined the otherwise modern summery look of the place. "Why don't you tell them to have off-white canvas slipcovers made," I suggested to the rental agent. "In a rental house?" she asked, horrified. But it's so practical because you just throw them into the washer and put them back on while still damp so they won't shrink and you don't have to iron. In this way the furniture always looks fresh and new.

White in the Bedroom

White suggests romance. Create the ambience of luxury by adding a bunch of sumptuous white pillows or pillows trimmed in white. Pillows with wide ruffles or flanges, scallop-edged shams, or European eyelet trim can all be combined to give any bed a dreamy quality.

White in the Kitchen

White streamlines a kitchen. If you are thinking about repainting the kitchen, go with white. I like a semigloss paint, or even a glaze finish to kitchen walls. It's easy to clean and makes everything seem new. White kitchen counters reflect light. For an interesting detail, edge the counters with a light stained wood. White dishes and bowls behind glass-front cabinets are refreshingly charming no matter how many times we see them displayed this way. Trim the front of shelves with a strip of paper doily edging. If small appliances like a coffee maker or a toaster are white, they will make the countertops seem less cluttered.

Dining in Style

Nothing is more elegant than a dinner table set with all white linens and chinaware. A white linen tablecloth sets the background, over which you might place a crocheted or lace cover in an eggshell shade. This will provide texture with the white background showing through. Creamware plates are lovely with damask napkins. In fact, white patterns of chinaware are classic and some never go out of style. Of all the tablewares, whites are usually the most economical. Add to this setting wooden, silver, or white ceramic candle holders with white candles and, in the center, a white pitcher, an aged basket to hold a pot of white primroses, or a bowl or clear glass vase with white tulips, a few freesia stems, white roses, or white lilacs. The greenery from the stems and leaves are all that's needed for a touch of color. Dress the sideboard with a white eyelet-edged runner.

White in the Bathroom

There is nothing more luxurious than huge, fluffy, white bath towels. Colorful towels just never seem as soft. This is because natural fibers left in their natural state grow softer with time. Roll up white hand towels and arrange them in an oversized natural reed basket. Almond or oatmeal soap in an antique dish can sit next to a small white creamer filled with a fresh bouquet. Add lovely extravagances like cutglass perfume bottles or a silver powder shaker. Lace-edged or sheer, white café curtains create a feeling of springtime freshness. Or try my trick: For an instant valance, fold lace, linen, or embroidered cocktail napkins on the diagonal over a curtain rod. Nothing could be simpler or nicer.

Collectible Accessories

Bleached wood picture and mirror frames, terra-cotta dishes lining the kitchen windowsill, a grouping of shells on a bathroom shelf, white creamers and pitchers in a breakfront, a soft mohair throw over the sofa, a fluffy white duvet, a teapot with cups and saucers: All set the stage for whatever else you might introduce. One of my favorites is a setting for tea: Wedgewood's basketweave china, white linen napkins, an antique white plate piled with tea sandwiches, and, of course, white sugar cubes in a silver holder.

IT'S EASY BEING GREEN

The late decorator Billy Baldwin once painted a room in a color he called magnolia leaf green. Against this dark green background he used the same color draperies and upholstery and, uncharacteristically, left out the stark white wood trim that we often see in his decorated rooms. The room succeeded, but could easily have failed if he had chosen different shades of green for each element.

Never make the mistake of assuming that all shades of the same color will work well together. When selecting a paint color, try to select shades of that color for fabric and other elements in the room and be sure they go together before beginning the project. Green is an interesting color when carefully used.

Rich Without Overpowering

If you want to create a strong, rich environment, use a dark inky green with dark woods like mahogany. Dark green is a good color for a study or a formal living room with high ceilings. For an early American look, many decorators favor Nantucket and Williamsburg green. Introduce black and cream for accents.

Tropical Green

Shades of aqua, turquoise, and celery green are marvelous in a sunroom or porch or in a vacation cottage. Large leafy prints on a stark white background look terrific on wicker and white painted furniture. Green and white are fresh and summery. A dining room in a soft celery green with white trim will look good anywhere in the country and in any style home. Always select your paint color two shades lighter than what you see on paint sample chips in the store. When applied to an entire room a color will always look much darker than on a tiny square.

Olive Green

Olive is a tricky shade of green to use, but can be quite interesting when accented with shades of yellow and white. In a room painted a slightly darker shade of green I have used a yellow-and-white checked chintz and lots of white trim and accessories. At the moment gold or gilding is very much "in" and looks wonderful against a deep green background. Use it sparingly as on a gilt-edged mirror or heavy frame, a table base, or candlesticks. A patterned rug with a light background and touches of green and yellow will enliven a green room.

Shades of Nature

I once decorated a beachside home in which every room had a spectacular view. One room was filled with windows on three sides. The view was all sea grass, low yellow shrubs, and sand dunes. I used a Waverly chintz fabric printed with small yellow buds and large green leaves that looked like airy palm fronds to cover cushions on a bamboo-frame sofa and chairs. The dark wooden floors were covered with a sand-colored area carpet. A dark-green wicker rocking chair had yellow-and-white striped chintz cushions, and a dark wooden Deacon's bench had a combination of the fabric pillows in different sizes. All the accessories related to the seashore. A collection of carved shore birds, lightship baskets, and shell boxes enhanced the theme. When you have a natural view, work with it to make the indoors and outdoors seamless.

Green and Lavender

Years ago I was in the Waverly showroom in Manhattan, where a room had been designed with shades of green and lavender. At first I thought it was terrible, but, as I studied it, the color combination began to grow on me. I found that, unlike some colors, almost any shade of green can work well with a shade of another color. We're used to seeing the color green. It appears everywhere in nature, and after a long barren winter, it gladdens us as the first sign of spring. I now use shades of lavender and purple with green in many ways. It's still unusual, if that's the look you're after. Try it in a baby's room. Just be sure to work out the shades and the fabrics before making the final commitment.

IN THE PINK

The only time I've seen pink work well as a paint color is in a bedroom. Even then, pink is a hard color to live with. It looks great when it first goes on, it makes people look all glowy and rosy, but after awhile we grow tired of it.

I once knew a woman who painted the hallway of her Federal-style home in bubble-gum pink. The grand, sweeping staircase was carpeted with black needlepoint and the floor was a black-and-white bold checkerboard design. But the pink didn't really work as well as intended. The only time pink makes sense is when a drop is added to white. It takes away the hospital stark-ness and gives the white a rosy softness. But pink is...well, pret-ty. So how can we use pink effectively in decorating without cre-ating a disaster? Try the following:

Roses Are Pink

An all-white sunroom with painted wicker looks wonderfully summery with pink-and-white striped fabric mixed with a soft rose print. The nice thing about pink is that you can mix and match all sorts of prints and they will look good together. Try pink rose-printed fabric for pillows with pink-and-white striped ruffles. Make a quilted patchwork throw from pink-and-white calico squares alternating with squares cut from pink rose prints. A small paint-ed blanket chest or side table might have a pink trim.

Pink Overhead

In tropical climates, the inside roof of an outdoor porch is often painted pale aqua, but pink would look just as nice. This is a soft touch that adds an element of surprise.

Dining in the Pink

Table linens in shades of pink help to create a pretty and invit-ing setting when entertaining. Pink dishes set a pleasant back-ground for food presentation. And, of course, pale pink flowers in a floral vase or dainty pitcher make the perfect centerpiece. Consider a pale pink linen tablecloth over which you place a smaller rose pink printed cloth. Use a variety of mixed napkins in different shades of pink and tie each with a pink ribbon. Insert a pink rose bud under each ribbon.

A Blush of Pink

A friend of mine wanted to paint her dining room red because she saw this done in a magazine. Her husband abhorred the idea. He wanted white. So they compromised and added a little red to a gallon of white and painted the walls what she called pink and he called coral. It worked. Everything looked rosy. There are many shades of pink and most will look good in a dining room.

Pink Carpets

Never! It simply doesn't work anywhere. Well, maybe in the bathroom for a little while. When my daughter wallpapered a bedroom with a pretty Ralph Lauren rose pattern on white, the room looked bright and inviting. The bare wood floors needed attention next. We brought home carpet samples ranging from white to deep rose. I thought a pale pink would work, picking up one of the rose colors in the paper. Even when we laid the small carpet sample on the floor we could tell that an entire room covered in pink would be dreadful. She opted for cream, just slightly darker than the background of the wallpaper and matching the woodwork trim around the room. Sometimes pink carpet can look soft and cozy in a small nursery. But wall-to-wall carpeting is a big investment and you don't want to have to replace it too often.

LET THE SUNSHINE IN

Yellow isn't a color that's been overused in decorating; however, many shades of yellow are perfect for different areas of the house, especially where you want to create a warm glow.

Choosing the Right Shade of Yellow

A pale shade of yellow can brighten a dark area and add more interest than white. Imagine opening a closet door to a burst of color! Bright yellow is a good choice here. When choosing a shade from a paint chip remember that colors look much lighter on a small sample than when applied to an entire wall. Choose a shade or two lighter than what you think you want. Be careful of a muddy yellow. The results will be the opposite of bright. The palest buttercup yellow is nice for a room that gets a lot of sunshine. The room will have a soft glow without being hot. It's a good choice for the nursery.

Cheerful Welcome

Yellow teamed with bright white makes an attractive and cheery color scheme. Consider a yellow-and-white striped wallpaper for an entryway. Add a warmly textured wood bench—such as pine—and soften it with a few yellow-and-white plaid pillows. Arrange gold-framed pictures or a mirror on the wall, or a row of coat pegs painted to match the yellow in the wallpaper.

Scandinavian Style

Yellow and blue with white is reminiscent of a Swedish country cottage à la designer Karl Larson. This is a pretty combination to use on fabrics and painted furniture in a vacation home or on a summer porch, deck, or patio. Fill white wicker chairs and chaise longues with pillows covered in a yellow and blue fabric, prints or solids. Ivy plants with dark green leaves are the perfect accent. Line them on top of an armoire or over kitchen cabinets and let the vines trail down. If you like this idea, a stenciled border of wispy vine and ivy leaves would be just right around a mirror, along a chair rail, or around a window or doorway.

A Touch of Color

Yellow doesn't have to be the dominant color. It can add character in small doses. For example, your walls might be painted dark green with white or beige trim. Choose a fabric with a small bit of yellow accent in it. Or, hang botanical or fruit prints over the sofa or in another prominent spot. A white ceramic bowl might hold lemons and limes on a sideboard, or use yellow accessories such as candleholders or pottery. Edge your curtains or drapes with a band of yellow fabric or use a yellow print as tiebacks on a solid curtain.

Comingling

If you use different shades of yellow with different prints in those shades, you can create a very interesting mix. Combine butterscotch with cream, peach, and sunny yellow. Plaids and checks work well with stripes and small prints. Soft furnishings made with shades of yellow work well with dark woods. Use lots of lush green plants for accent. Sisal and natural wicker are good textures. You can add a touch of another color any time you want a change. For example, something lavender will keep the tone, but will add an unusual touch.

 # GOLDEN RULE

In the 1930s and 1940s people in this country often had gilding removed from their antiques as a response to an "embarrassment of riches." In the 1960s you couldn't give away gilded furniture. Those who had it painted over it. Now, in the 1990s, gold is making a comeback. Gold-leaf wallpaper, at $150 a yard, might not be in everyone's budget, nor an eighteenth-century gilt wood console for twenty-five thousand dollars, but gold leafing and gilding is definitely having an effect on current decorating inspiration.

A Gold-and-White Theme

Clothing designer Donna Karen has a house in the Hamptons on Long Island that is furnished with a gold-and-white scheme. Decorators who are using gold explain that it represents luxury in decorating. Gold-edged chinaware is making a comeback as well. White china with a simple gold rim is the classic wedding gift. Gold braid trim can be found on bed linens and pillows, and you'll even find golden taffeta dust ruffles in better linen departments. Water-gilded frames, moldings, and chair frames are back in style. So if you have such an inherited piece, hang onto it and don't give it a coat of paint.

A Little Goes a Long Way

Always in style is the gilt-frame mirror. A real antique like the one you may have inherited from a distant aunt might be worth thousands. On the other hand, a new one can be found for under two hundred dollars and will give a room the same feeling of opulence. Look for small items such as candlesticks and gold-rimmed glasses for setting a golden table. Placemats and tablecloths are available with a gold trim, or you can add gold braid to any fabric accessory to give it an updated look.

Do-It-Yourself

In response to this trend there is a revival of the ancient craft of gilding. This craft comes in and out of favor quickly, and only among those who really enjoy such a challenge. It is not for the impatient crafter because it is terribly labor intensive. It takes a great deal of practice to apply it with the sort of skill that would render it acceptable beyond application on a frame, for example.

If you'd like to try your hand at it, take a tip from the experts who suggest taking a class because the process is too complicated to learn by experimentation. However, for those of you who might like to add a little gold trim to an inexpensive frame or around a painted box, you can have some fun with a new product from the Formby's Decorative Touches line. They make a gold leaf pen for home crafters. And for those who want the look of opulence but can't afford to gold-leaf the dining room ceiling, play a trick on yourself and use gold spray paint on a yard-sale find. You'll be right in style.

COLORFUL INTRODUCTIONS

After a colorless winter we often react to the arrival of spring with a desire to add bright colors to both the inside of a home and the outdoor living spaces. The following "bright ideas" might help you introduce colors in small areas to change the look of a room without a lot of effort.

Cheerful Welcoming!

Create a bold entryway floor with a deep hunter green and cream-colored checkerboard floor pattern. You can achieve this with large squares of tile or by painting the floor. Add a painted bench or sideboard in bright yellow or red, and hang colorful framed pictures along the wall. Or, paint a strip of wall pegs for holding hats or coats above the bench.

Punchy Porch

Give a coat of a bright color stain or paint to a wooden window box and hang it on the inside of the railing. You might want several. If you have a deck without a fence or railing, line the colorful boxes around the floor rim and fill with flowering plants.

Pillow Power!

White linen sofas and chairs come alive with the addition of colorful pillows. Choose a variety of bright fabric pillows that go together, but aren't necessarily matching. If you make your own, mix and match with a contrasting piping on each. Highlight photographs or colorful prints with colored matting and frame them in painted frames for a grouping over the sofa. This small accessory of color will change the scene instantly. A vase of flowers, colorful valances, and a painted floorcloth or throw rug ties it all together and these accessories are easy to remove when you're tired of color.

Quick Country Kitchen

It's easy to brighten a kitchen with a country look. Begin with red-and-white or blue-and-white plaid linen dishtowels for no-sew café curtains. Next, paint the tops of unfinished bar stools bright red or blue to match the curtains. Paint the stool legs white for a bold contrast. Then buy or paint a group of cannisters to match and display them on the counter. Start pots of herbs in a painted metal window box on the kitchen windowsill.

Fancy Facade!

An exterior window that faces a patio or deck area can be spruced up in no time with a little paint, a stencil design, and a decorative window box. Use a precut ivy design around the window frame and stencil it with exterior, waterproof latex paint to look as though ivy is "growing" around the window. This paint is easy to apply and easy to clean up. Next, add a painted window box and fill it with colorful pots of flowers and some ivy trailing over the edges and down the front to look like an extension of the stencil design.

All Decked Out!

Create a colorful oasis with stain and paint on furniture and planters. Thompson's Water Seal now makes more than one hundred different outdoor opaque and semi-transparent stain colors. Use a combination of citrus colors on Adirondack chairs and make a grouping of colorful flower pots. Paint a little wooden occasional table with exterior paint so it can be left outdoors, then add whimsical dots, dashes, and squiggles in freehand. Fruit-print fabric pillows can rest in each chairback.

Fresh as a Daisy!

Create a fresh-as-a-daisy dining area with a green, yellow, and blue color scheme. Add a yellow-and-blue area rug on a painted floor, a green painted table and chairs, yellow-and-green fabric covers, a hanging plant, lemons in a blue ceramic bowl, and pretty matted and framed pictures.

Floors

 # CARPET KNOW-HOW

What kind of carpet should I put in which room? Can a carpet make a large room cozier or a small room seem bigger? Can carpeting make a dark room lighter? And what happens if you order wall-to-wall carpeting and find it's all wrong—after it's installed? Here are some room-by-room tips from The Carpet and Rug Institute for buying carpets.

High Traffic

The dining room, family room, hallways, and stairs are high-traffic areas. Here you'll want stain resistance. Durable saxonie is a good example of a practical carpet. It's made with yarns of two or more ply twisted together and heat-set to lock in twist so each tuft is visible in the surface.

The Living Room

This is the area that you want to show off. Lush, cut pile velvets and plushes are luxurious if the living room isn't the one you also use as a family room.

Bedrooms

This is your own private place. Make it a place that is soothing and relaxing. Pamper yourself with a carpet that is deep and plush and makes you happy to get up in the morning.

Patterns

I usually shy away from carpet patterns because we tire of them faster than a solid color. Borders, however, work well on area carpets in a living room or den, especially against beautiful wood floors. I learned about patterns the hard way. I chose a subtle brown-on-beige shell pattern for wall-to-wall carpeting in my den. I live on an island. I thought this would be an appropriate theme for this small room. I've had it a year. I'm tired of looking at it. A few stubborn spots of dirt have taken up permanent residence between the dark shells, which makes the entire symmetrical pattern look weird. I'm waiting for it to get really unbearable to look at before changing it to a salt-and-pepper pattern that hides ground-in Cheerios.

Color

A carpet's color should work with the other elements in the room—furniture, paint or wallpaper colors and patterns, paintings or artwork on the walls, window treatments, etc.—and will definitely influence the overall mood of the room.

A light color is relaxing in a bedroom. But most of all, choose colors that you're comfortable with. Never choose a color because it's the "flavor of the month." If you carpet your living room in red because it looked good in a current decorating magazine, you might not love it so much a few months later.

Dark colors tend to show dirt, animal hairs, lint, etc., more than light colors. A deep green, for example can be very rich looking in a living room but totally impractical in a den. A friend of mine who's a decorator carpeted her living room in black. It looked sensational and very dramatic with her glass and chrome furniture. But it turned out to be a nightmare because it showed every single piece of dust, lint, and light dirt particles that blew through the room. The carpet never looked as good as it had in the showroom. She has since moved and did not take the carpet with her.

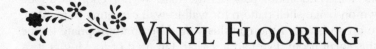

VINYL FLOORING

When it comes to floor covering for bathrooms and kitchens, you have lots of options. Tile can be expensive although it's always great in a bathroom. But if you haven't taken a look at what's new in vinyl floor covering you might be surprised. Vinyl resilient floor covering has come a long way and it's a good solution for many areas of the home.

I was recently in a well-known architect's house where he had used the new Congoleum vinyl throughout every room. All the walls were painted white and the floor was a continuous periwinkle blue. The effect was gorgeous. Here's the up-to-date scoop on vinyl.

For a Hall

An extremely elegant and modern sheet vinyl from Congoleum is their Futura "Regal Crest." It looks like ceramic tiles with contrasting diamond insets between each tile. I like the Midnight Black with Polar White diamonds, but you might like Midnight Green or one of the other colors. It's perfect for a large entrance hallway.

For the Bathrooms

If you'd like to have the look of marble tile but can't afford it, the solution is "Roman Elegance," which is a dramatic design with the look of 12 × 12-inch slabs of luxurious marble. It comes in six colors, but my preference is Midnight Green.

Another design, "Plaza Suite," is quite lovely if you want the look of natural stone. Each square tile design is 6 × 6 inches and comes in soft colors like pale blue or muslin.

For the Family Room

"Santa Fe" is a large-scale design that gives the effect of classic 12 × 12-inch Southwestern saltillo tile. It comes in six wonderful earth tones like Clay Terra Cotta and Clay Burnt Umber. This tile would be great in a kitchen as well.

For the Kitchen

Congoleum has a design called "Royal Gallery" that's practical and good looking in a kitchen. It's a 12 × 12-inch "tile" design with a repeat of four diamond insets. Each of the squares is a slightly different shade of the same color and has a mottled look with some depth to it, much like marble. This pattern is especially good for high-traffic areas.

Installation

Congoleum's Futura line of vinyl floor covering is six feet wide, which minimizes waste. Best of all it can be put down over an existing vinyl floor. Check with a knowledgeable person at your home center so you get all the tools you need if you are doing this yourself.

Good Points

The Futura flooring is easy to clean and won't scratch, dull, scuff, or stain. It's pretty thick so it's comfortable to stand on, in a kitchen for example, when preparing meals. For kids' rooms or the family room it's extremely quiet. The Futura line runs about forty-six dollars a square yard.

About Linoleum

Now getting back to the old days....Linoleum was a hard, smooth flooring made from a solidified mixture of linseed oil and ground cork laid on a backing of canvas or burlap. It was more durable than canvas floorcloths and it was easier to clean. Linoleum was a practical choice for people many years ago if they couldn't afford the luxury of wood, marble, or ceramic flooring.

Some Quick Facts

It wasn't until the late 1950s that Congoleum introduced twelve-foot-wide sheet vinyl floor coverings, and it wasn't until the 1960s that the first "no wax" vinyl floor coverings appeared. In the 1970s we got stain- and mildew-resistance; in the 1980s Congoleum introduced a vinyl floor inlaid with pearlescent vinyl chips to give a dimensional look as well as a high gloss, urethane finish that's scuff resistant. As if all this weren't enough, the company now makes its products with mildew protection, a satin-gloss finish, and added traction when wet so you won't break your neck while carrying your groceries in on a rainy day.

Consumer Information

For more information on where to get vinyl tiling, how to install it, or anything else you want to know, call Congoleum's toll-free hotline: 1-800-934-3567.

Just Like Wood

If you want the look of wood, but the carefree maintenance of vinyl, consider wood grain-patterned vinyl from Pergo. It comes in eight-inch by four-foot lengths and in all different wood grain patterns.

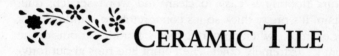 # CERAMIC TILE

Ceramic tile is functional and good looking. Whether your style is country, colonial, or contemporary there's a color, texture, size, and style tile for the situation. Ceramic tile is durable, it won't dent, cut, burn, dull, or stain. It's virtually maintenance free. Just damp-mop it to keep the floor looking great.

In an Entryway

American Olean offers a selection of glazed floor tile that looks like natural stone or rich marble, to name just two types. Either of these would be sensational for a first impression in the hallway. The semigloss surface resists stains and scratches. It won't fade or discolor. I like the deep green marble look of the 11^3/$_4$-inch squares.

Another idea is to use two different tile colors such as black-and-white Stonestyles to create a dramatic statement. These tiles look like natural marble and come in 11³/₄-inch squares. You might also like the warm tones of rose and linen or the cool grays.

In the Bathroom

Combine polished and unpolished tile for the bathroom. Friends of mind are remodeling an old fifties-style bathroom and putting in a Jacuzzi as well as stall shower. For the floor they're using unpolished tile called Terra Pavers, made by American Olean Tile Company. Terra Pavers have a contemporary granite look and are almost twelve inches square. They will use the polished tiles for the sides of the tub and for the walls of the shower stall. These tiles are excellent for floors, walls, countertops, and backsplashes.

Outdoor Patio and Pool Areas

Unglazed quarry tiles are inviting and warm with a natural, rich color throughout. They come in earth tones like fawn gray, sahara, canyon red, and umber. They are 6 × 6 inches and would look terrific around a pool or as a patio. They are also quite handsome in an entryway.

In the Kitchen

It's easy to be creative by combining tiles with borders around the floor as well as on the backsplash. There's a lot to choose from, including florals, geometrics, or solid colors. If you haven't visited a tile store lately, you'll be amazed at the elaborate and extensive variety to choose from. There you'll find reproductions of Old World European tile patterns as well as contemporary styles.

In the Dining Room

More and more frequently we see tile being used in dining rooms. A nice glazed tile in solid colors is durable, stain and scratch resistant, and often more interesting than a carpet. In fact you can define the area where you will place your table and chairs by creating a border with a tile that contrasts with those used on the rest of the floor. For example, American Olean has a glazed tile called Creekstones that comes in chalk, sand, gray slate, rose, azure blue, and terra-cotta. Each tile is 8⁵/₈-inches, and the colors all work nicely together to create a carpetlike pattern.

Custom Looks

Tile is good looking wherever it's used. It can enhance a staircase, totally change an entryway, modernize an old kitchen, and add a custom look to the bathroom.

Fabric Matches

Now you can even coordinate tile patterns with your fabrics. Laura Ashley has designed a collection of tile to match their classic country patterns. So you can outfit your bathroom with curtains, shower curtain, and tiles to match for a really coordinated look. For example, you can use one of their wallpaper borders to create a chair rail around the bathroom, then add large tile squares in a color to match. Laura Ashley tile is manufactured by American Olean.

WOODEN IT BE LOVERLY

Wood floors can be finished in a variety of ways depending on the look you want and the way you use each room.

Bare All

Few people put down a wood floor only to cover it with carpeting. However, there are areas that need softening and, in these, area carpets can be used. Also, bare floors are cold and carpeting muffles sound. To protect a new floor, apply two or three coats of polyurethane. If you want the floors to have a warm honey tone, use an oil-based finish. To avoid a yellow cast to the wood, choose a water-base finish. The water base dries in about an hour and you can easily apply two or three coats in one day.

In a Pickle

A whitewashed cast to the floors is often desireable when you want a light and airy finish on your floors. There are many pickling stains on the market made especially for this purpose. You can protect the wood and stain it at the same time. Many vacation homes have white pickled floors, and the effect is summery and fresh. I've even seen this treatment on porches and decks. By using a transparent white deck stain and water seal, you can give your outdoor wood floors a water-resistant finish with a white cast.

Painted Floors

Old floors of no particular interest can be sanded and painted in a color that goes with your decorating scheme. This treatment was particularly popular in early American homes where soft pine was often used. White was the color of choice, but I've seen painted floors in all different colors. A painted checkerboard floor treatment is especially attractive and often used in hallway areas. Large squares of black and white or deep green and white are the favorite combinations. However, in areas where you might want a pattern that isn't overwhelming or too bold, such as in a bathroom or bedroom, use a soft cream and white. This is subtle, but every bit as dramatic.

Spatter Paint

Another painted floor treatment is spatter painting. After a floor is painted a solid color, you can spatter it with a contrasting color or a multitude of colors. It's easy to do and can be a practical way to treat a child's room or family room.

Stenciled

 Whether you choose to paint or polyurethane the floors, you can add interest with a stenciled border around the outside edge where the floor meets the walls. You'll find precut border stencils in a variety of designs. A geometric pattern might be nice in a dining room or formal living room, while a weaving vine would be pretty on a

bathroom floor. Some stencil designs call for one color only, while others require several colors. Decide which will suit your scheme best and plan it out on paper before beginning the project. For protection, apply a coat of polyurethane over the finished stencil border.

Protection for Hardwood Floors

"Solid hardwood floors repay a little care with a lifetime of value," says the Hardwood Manufacturers Association. Solid hardwood floors give a room richness, warmth, and natural beauty. All floors need regular care. Sweep, vacuum, or dust-mop at least once a week. Here are some tips:

1. Dirt, grit, and sand act like sandpaper on the finish, causing scratches, dents, and dulling. Place floor mats at entrances to trap dirt and prevent damage.
2. Standing water can warp a poorly finished hardwood floor and damage the finish. Simply wipe up all spills as they happen.
3. Avoid oil soaps. They can build up and create problems when it's time to put a maintenance coat on the floor. Instead, neutral pH cleaners made specifically for wood floors are recommended.
4. Lift furniture, don't drag it. Self-adhesive felt contacts under the legs will help prevent scratches.
5. Vacuum with a dust attachment, don't use vacuums with beater bars.
6. Direct sun can discolor hardwood floors. Close curtains and blinds or add sheet drapes to protect from the sun's intense UV rays.
7. Canister vacuums with special bare-floor attachments are the surest way to get rid of all dirt and dust.
8. Use a good dust mop, one with a 12- to 18-inch cotton head and a special dust mop treatment. Spray the treatment onto the mop head 12 to 24 hours before dust mopping.

Old Hardwood Floors

If you installed hardwood floors a few years ago and they now look old, what can you do about it? Before you do anything, check the condition of the finish and the wood to see whether they need special cleaning or more involved repair.

The Water Test

Has the finish been worn off or is it just dirty? To test if the finish has worn off, begin in a high-traffic area and pour one to two tablespoons of water onto the floor. If the water soaks in immediately and leaves a darkened spot, the finish is worn and any water can damage the wood. If the water soaks in after a few minutes and darkens the wood only slightly, the finish is partially worn. If the water beads on top, the surface is properly sealed. Repeat this test in low- and medium-traffic areas.

Wood Condition

If the finish is worn, the wood may have been damaged. Are there stains, burns, cuts, gouges, holes, cracks, or warped boards? If the wood is damaged, repair or replacement may be required before deep-cleaning your floor.

Surface Finishes

Nearly all floors installed today have surface finishes, mostly polyurethane. They are often glossy and may look like a layer of clear plastic on top of the wood. A small amount of paint remover in an inconspicuous area of the floor will cause the surface to bubble (unless it's a water-based urethane, which will cause no reaction).

Penetrating Seals

Oils and waxes usually have a satin or matte finish. If you can feel the wood grain when you run your hand across the surface, it's most likely a penetrating seal. Paint remover will have no effect on it, but wax stripper or ammonia will soften and whiten the surface.

Cleaning

The fastest and best way to deep-clean solid hardwood floors is damp mopping. Dip the mop in a neutral pH wood cleaner and water, wring it out so it's about half-dry, and go over the floor. Dip the mop into clean water, wring it as dry as you can, and mop over the floor again.

Vinegar, often recommended to clean hardwood floors, does nothing for removing grease and soil.

Waxing Pros and Cons

Pro: Wax can be easily cleaned, buffed, and rewaxed to make it look like its original condition. Wear and tear will be on the wax, not the finish. It's easily stripped and reapplied. *Con:* Waxing may limit some refinishing and recoating options down the road. If not properly stripped, the wax can cause adhesion problems when recoating the surface. Only wax a surface finish if the original finish is in poor shape and you don't plan to refinish your floor in the near future.

Stain Removal from Waxed Floors

1. Water Stains: Rub the spot with No. 2 steel wool and rewax. For more serious water stains, lightly sand with fine sandpaper, clean the spot with No. 1 or 00 steel wool and mineral spirits or floor cleaner, then refinish and wax.
2. Cigarette Burns: If not severe, the burn can be removed by rubbing with steel wool moistened with soap and water.
3. Heel and Caster Marks: Rub vigorously with fine steel wool and floor cleaner. Wipe dry and polish.
4. Ink Stains and Other Dark Spots: Use No. 2 steel wool and floor cleaner to clean the spot and surrounding area. Thoroughly wash the affected area. If the spot remains, sand with fine sandpaper, rewax, and polish. Stubborn stains may require that you replace the affected area.
5. Chewing Gums and Wax Deposits: Ice until the deposit is brittle and crumbles off. Pour floor cleaner around the stain so the fluid soaks under and loosens it.
6. Alcohol Spots: Rub the spot with liquid or paste wax.
7. Repairing Wax Finishes: Rub fine steel wool in a puddle of reconditioner or paint thinner and clean as you go. Apply wax and buff.
8. Tip: Always start cleaning at the edge of a stain and work toward the center so it won't spread.

Squeaks

When the air in your home becomes extremely dry, your floor will lose moisture and contract. Conversely, when humidity is high, your floor will absorb moisture and expand slightly. As humidity stabilizes, hardwoods regain their original dimensions. Air-conditioning in summer and humidifying in winter will keep your home's humidity comfortable for you and your floor. To silence squeaks: Apply liquid wax, powdered soap, talcum powder, or powdered graphite between floorboards that are rubbing together. If that doesn't stop the squeak, drive two-inch finishing nails through pilot holes on both edges of the board then hide the hole with putty or wax of a matching color.

For More Information

If you have any questions about hardwood you can call the Hardwood Manufacturers Association at (800) 373-WOOD. Or you can send for their free 12-page illustrated booklet called "How to Care for Solid Hardwood Floors" by writing to: HMA, Department NE295, 400 Penn Center Boulevard, Suite 350, Pittsburgh, Pennsylvania 15235.

Windows

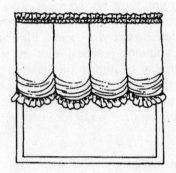

WINDOW SHADES

When I first moved into a new home the first thing that became obvious was how many windows I had to deal with. Most homes have lots of windows, and even if you have no intention of treating them to fancy drapes and curtains right away, you will need something to cover them for privacy. One of the easiest and most practical solutions is to use the same window treatment throughout the house. This makes the house look good from the outside, and will save you a lot of trouble. That is, of course, if you can find something that works for every room.

Shades

The world of shades has gotten so enormous that if you haven't been in a home-furnishings store in a long time you will be amazed at what's available. There is everything from the discount store roll-up shade and mini blinds to elaborate made-to-order fabric shades. Horizontal and vertical blinds are always classic, but wood slat blinds are making a big comeback. These aren't the old-fashioned Venetian blinds of yore, but contemporary wood blinds in different widths and a variety of different colors. They're handsome and very much "of the moment" in their new incarnation. Definitely worth checking out.

Fabric Shades

Soft fabric shades are enjoying a renaissance. You'll find everything from billowy Austrian shades and the less voluminous balloon shade, to the Roman shade, which draws up in folds rather than poufs and has a more tailored appearance. This shade is quite popular because it works well with or without a swag, drapery, or valance overtreatment and has a more pared-down look for today's interiors.

Vignette

The Hunter Douglas company has a version of the Roman shade, called Vignette. It has layers of gently contoured fabric folds affixed to a rear fabric panel. The layers overlap one another like waves and, when raised, disappear into a sleek curved headrail. All unsightly gathering or stacking is eliminated. When lowered, Vignette provides privacy and sun protection but still allows light to come through. It operates smoothly with a single cord loop, and from the outside the window looks like it's covered with a sheer curtain. It's a neat solution for most window problems. The company has lots of other styles and you can find out where to see them in your area by calling 1-800-937-STYLE (937-7895).

Plain Shades

If all you want is a cheap roller shade until you get around to "doing" each window, don't be locked into conventional hanging. Remember that shades can be placed at half mast or where you'd put a café curtain if you want to keep the top half of the window clear. I have a friend who reversed the shade so it could be pulled up from the bottom of the window and hook at the top. This was because he didn't want to cover the entire window when he needed privacy only at street level.

Duette

This is a honeycomb pleated shade from Hunter Douglas and is made of fabrics that look like raw silk, textured linen, or satin. They come translucent or opaque. The pleats hold their shape permanently, and if you have a narrow window molding this is a good solution because it's rather sleek. The pleats are of half-inch construction with a half-inch headrail and an even sleeker bottom rail. It comes in more than three hundred colors.

REVIEWING WINDOWS

Many years ago I was hired as a consultant to a large company that manufactured window curtains, drapes, and shades. The owner was a nuts-and-bolts kind of fellow who reasoned that everyone had lots of windows and needed to cover them in some way, so how could he miss? He made plain inexpensive curtains for a low-end price scale, but after thirty or more years in the business aspired to a more upscale approach so he could get his goods into the better department stores. The gap between his approach, something cheap to give privacy, and mine, something attractive to enhance a room, was too great for a long-term relationship. So my dabbling in the world of mass market was quickly terminated.

Reasons for Window "Treatments"

Mr. Mass Market curtains didn't know about the word "treatments," as used by decorating magazines to describe what you do to decorate windows.

1. If your home is surrounded by neighbors, you need some kind of window covering for privacy.
2. Soft fabric drapes serve as noise deterents soaking up ambient sound.
3. Draperies add to the warmth and charm of the decor. At night, black window panes are unattractive and pulling drapes over them is often preferable.

Formal Treatment

For a formal room, install a shade, then a sheer curtain panel over which you'll have heavier side panels, and finally a valance that might be sleek and contemporary or elaborately pleated, draped, or ruffled. These treatments require all sorts of double and triple rods engineered to hold one set of fabrics over another, and each operates on its own system. They are available at all decorating and fabric shops.

Simply Stated

I like plain, unadorned windows with plain, unadorned shades that do what they are supposed to do: give me privacy at night. Shades are easy to install, they are the least obtrusive window covering, and they are relatively carefree. They are also fairly inexpensive and can be replaced when they get unsightly. But there are shades and there are shades.

The Hunter Douglas company has introduced Applause™ Honeycomb shades. They are good-looking, inexpensive, easy-to-care-for, and easy-to-install window shades. It's impossible to wade through a large collection of window styles to decide what would be best for each of your windows in every room. A uniform system that works in every situation is ideal. The honeycomb shades come in seventy-two different styles and colors from a translucent linenlike fabric in a three-eighths-inch pleat and thirty colors to a three-quarters-inch pleat and a blackout fabric in twelve tones. To find out who sells Hunter Douglas shades in your area, call 1-800-937-STYLE (937–7895).

One Choice, Many Ways

It often makes sense to use the same window treatment on all your windows. There is a consistency of design throughout, and from the outside the house looks better with all windows treated identically. It really simplifies things when decorating a home.

If you're still of the school that says a room isn't complete without curtains, you can always add whatever fabric treatment you want over the shades. However, keep it simple. As with all overdone decorating, you can quickly become bored with an elaborate window treatment; with shades, you always have privacy and a finished look or a good beginning.

Walls

WHAT ABOUT WALLS?

Do your walls give away the era in which you last decorated your house? Sometimes we live with wallpaper or a paint color for so long we no longer see it. Something isn't quite right, but we don't pay much attention and no matter how you rearrange the furniture over the years the room doesn't look fresh and new.

There are all sorts of ways to update a room by tackling the walls. The following suggestions might help.

Molding

Dating back to Roman times, molding can still work wonders for any room. Simply installing elegant crown moldings, chair rails, or base molds can give a room a whole new look for a reasonable price.

Wood Paneling

The natural warmth of real wood paneling can change the entire character of a room. In fact, it will add character where none exists. For example, install rustic Millplank or Barnplank paneling from Georgia-Pacific to add a country flair. Or, consider a classic beaded paneling look, which we often see in seaside homes. All are available from home centers nationwide.

Wainscoting

This is paneling that spans the bottom half of a wall, capped off by a chair rail. This adaptable design can dress up any room.

Either cut a 4 × 8-foot piece of paneling in thirds to 32 inches high, or use precut wainscoting panels.

Judges Paneling

The stately elegance of this paneling, found in movie classics and old-time libraries, is perfect for a den. Georgia Pacific has a booklet called "Build It Better with Hardwood Plywood" that shows how to create a design by combining hardwood, plywood, matching grain lumber, and real wood molding. This booklet is part of their "Great Possibilities" series and you can get it for $3 by writing to Georgia-Pacific Corp. P.O. Box 1763, Norcross, GA 30091. Be sure to state the name of the booklet.

Painting

Faux finishes are big right now and it's easy to marbleize, sponge, or rag your walls right over the existing paint. There are lots of books on painting techniques. I especially like *Recipes for Surfaces* (by Mindy Drucker, Simon & Schuster, 1990), which I've had for a long time in anticipation of glazing my bathroom walls.

Wallpaper

I love to wallpaper, but only if it's the prepasted kind, which is limiting. All the best wallpaper needs paste. But there's still plenty out there that comes prepasted, and if you don't have the inclination to do a faux painted finish, Waverly has a line of faux-finish wallpaper that is really terrific. I've used it a lot and everyone thinks I painted the walls. Maybe this is because I have a reputation for doing that sort of thing. In reality I do only what I can do easily, quickly, and in a way that I think will produce more foolproof results than doing it another way.

Borders

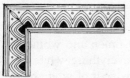 If hanging paper is a hassle, just add a border around the room. Or add a border of a stencil design. When you tire of it, paint it out. However, there are wallpaper borders that come with a peel-off backing for self-stick that can be easily removed. A border over the backsplash in a kitchen or bathroom is just about the easiest and most

effective way to upgrade these rooms. Adding a wallpaper border around windows or door molding is another way to decorate. The 3M Company makes kits for decorating children's rooms with peel-away borders and add-ons that work like Colorforms. These will not mess up the walls. Look for them in home centers nationwide.

Tile

Use tile in the same way to create a border. Consider applying painted tiles as a chair rail in the kitchen, or around a mirror in the bathroom.

Small Space, Big Impact

If papering or painting an entire room seems too big a commit-ment, consider doing one wall in a room. By papering one wall you can visually create interest and separate spaces without adding walls. Use the same wallpaper somewhere else in the room to tie it together. For example, use it as a border or to cover a win-dow cornice.

Rearrangement

If you're definitely not into doing any of the above, take down all the paintings, framed pictures, and mirrors in your house and use them to create a wall collage. Reserve one wall for family pho-tographs and change the arrangement with the seasons.

PAINTING KNOW-HOW

The most common do-it-yourself job for both men and women is painting. A friend of mine likes to paint everything white and every spring she gives all her furniture a new coat of white paint. This year she's redoing her kitchen. She doesn't care if the job is done neatly, only that it gets done. However, if you'd rather do it right the first time, here are some tips from the paint expert at Builder's Square.

Prepare the Surface

Preparation includes sanding and priming. You shouldn't have any glossy surfaces. The shiny areas should be roughed up with sandpaper to ensure proper adhesion of the new paint. Also, old paint should be thoroughly scraped so that all loose chips are knocked free of the surface; otherwise, the loose chip will break off with the fresh paint.

Use a proper primer for unfinished wood, drywall, or plaster. The thin primer coat helps the finished coat adhere to the surface. Always prime any latex surface that is to be covered with oil-based paint. If you are making a significant color change, then a white primer will help cover the old color.

Get Tough

Toughen up the rough areas. Sometimes drywalls have small cracks and holes. Fill them with putty or spackle. Let it dry, then sand it smooth.

Paneling

Don't paint over interior paneling that isn't solid wood. The high gloss will repel the paint and cheaper grades of paneling will buckle and disintegrate from wet paint.

Getting Ready

Take everything off the walls and put your furniture in the middle of the room. Don't scrimp on plastic drop cloth to cover your possessions. It tends to tear when spread out. Use a plastic cover of one millimeter thickness that's tough enough to stretch and shed paint droplets.

Mask It Out

Mask windows, doors, and other areas you won't be painting. Now's the time to use the thinner plastic. It can be cut to size and taped to cover windows and doors. Or you can use newspaper for this. Several companies make special rolls of reusable masking tape with adhesive on only one edge of the tape.

Clean Up

Vacuum the room before painting so the dust you stir up won't settle on the wet paint. Wipe the walls as well and scrub surfaces to be painted.

Selecting Paint

Paint with special qualities has been developed for spray painters. Shop for quality. A cheaper paint may not have the same ability to adhere to the surface as a better one. You may have to apply an extra coat to get the coverage you want, which will end up costing as much as or more than had you used a better brand.

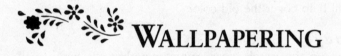 # WALLPAPERING

The most common mistake when wallpapering is the most frustrating: running out of paper before you finish the job. It doesn't hurt to buy an extra roll, since unopened rolls can be returned. Also, every print run is assigned a number and sometimes the same print, bought at another time, may not match in color exactly. The easiest wallpaper to hang is one that is prepasted. The pattern with the least amount of waste is a random nonrepeat pattern that matches edge to edge.

Tips for Accurate Measuring

There are a few simple steps to follow in order to calculate the exact amount of square footage that needs to be covered.

1. Determine the room's perimeter by measuring the width of all the walls and adding those figures together.
2. Measure the height of the room, less the width of baseboards or crown molding.
3. Multiply the total perimeter (step 1) times the height (step 2) for the total square footage of the room.
4. Determine the square footage of the areas in the room that will

not be covered by the wallpaper, such as doors, windows, etc., and total them.

5. Subtract the figure in step 4 from the total square footage in step three to come up with the square footage that needs to be covered with wallpaper.
6. If you plan to cover the ceiling, multiply its length times its width.
7. Then add the wall and ceiling figures together for a total.

Example

A room 15 × 10 feet has a perimeter of 50 feet (15 + 15 + 10 + 10 = 50). The walls are 8 feet high with 6-inch baseboards and 6-inch crown moldings (8 − 1/2 − 1/2 = 7 feet). Multiply the perimeter times the height for a total of 350 square feet. If the room has a window 3 × 4 = 12 and one door 3 × 7 = 21, then add these figures together for a total of 33 square feet in doors and windows (12 + 21 = 33). Subtract 33 from 350 to determine that you will need

317 square feet to cover the walls in the room. If you are covering the ceiling, too, then add 150 square feet (15 × 10 = 150) for a total of 467 square feet to cover with wallpaper.

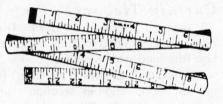

Double-Check

Measure the room twice to double-check. Take the measurements to the wallpaper store and have the person there compute the number of rolls you'll need of the paper you choose. On large patterns that demand repeat match, figure on about 10 percent waste. On smaller patterns where the repeat is more than 12 inches apart, add an extra half-roll. There will also be a little waste because most 8-foot sections need an additional 2 inches at the top and bottom for installation.

WALLPAPER BORDERS

From time to time I appear on television programs when the producers want a segment on weekend decorating. My demonstrations usually involve showing how the audience can solve decorating problems quickly, easily, and usually inexpensively. I try to introduce clever ideas as well. One of the items I like to work with is wallpaper borders. There are many designs in many different widths, and it's fun to come up with new ways to use them, aside from the obvious application on walls.

Curtain Tiebacks

Last year I appeared on *Oprah*. During the filming in my own home, I had planned to show how one might use wide French ribbon (the kind with wire in the edges) to fashion curtain tiebacks without a stitch. However, I couldn't find the ribbon I needed and quickly found another solution that worked surprisingly well . . . wallpaper border. The architectural motif in Thibaut's "Roman" border made it a refreshing accent to a plain white drapery. You simply cut the length you need, turn down the raw ends, and attach a clip-on curtain ring to each end. Wrap it around the curtain at the desired place and attach the rings to a hook on the wall. It's quite good looking. Choose a color and pattern to suit your room. I used a rich green.

Floorcloth

Another of my projects was making a floorcloth. This has become quite popular as a decorative item and you can easily make one to fit any room or space. It's made of artist's canvas (available at art supply stores) that comes on rolls. You cut the canvas to the desired size, and it can then be painted in any color. I chose to sponge glaze the background with Formby's Sponging Glaze Mix and Accent paint in a mauve pink. Once covered, the edges can then be finished with a wallpaper border. For this I used the same Thibaut "Roman" border in a rose color to offset my floorcloth, but match my tie-backs. Cut strips of wallpaper for each side of the floorcloth and miter the corners before glueing in place. Once dry, apply a coat or two of clear varnish finish over all to protect it. When this dries you can walk on it and sponge it clean when it gets dirty.

Tabletops

There's a wallpaper border that's a classic design in the Laura Ashley Home Furninshing's line called Charlotte in cowslip yellow and blue on a white background. I especially like this four and a half inch border for a tabletop. The table I used for this project was an unfinished country farm table from Mastercraft. It's sturdy and good-looking and lends itself to all sorts of interesting finishes. Paint, pickle, or stain the top of any dining table. Cut the wallpaper border strips to go around the table and glue in position with regular Elmer's glue. Then apply several coats of clear waterbase finish (which dries in about a half hour), allowing each coat to dry before applying the next. If your table is painted white, the water varnish won't yellow the paint the way oil-base varnish will.

Kids' Rooms

There are many little ways to add decorative touches to a nursery with wallpaper borders. Don't think you have to do a big job for big impact. For example, Laura Ashley Home Furnishings has an adorable line of wallpaper borders that would be perfect on the front of dresser drawers. In particular, one called "Ducks" features a continuous row of ducks in a field of yellow daffodils. The mostly green, yellow, and blue colors are as delightful and can be used right over their "Canasta Check" wallpaper, which is a yellow-and-white plaid, or on a painted wall just above the crib or youth bed. "Humpty-Dumpty" is another design in primary colors and "Hens," which is perfect for a toddlers's room.

Windows

Wallpaper borders are wonderful treatments around windows. They can make a small window look larger, give an uninteresting window character, accentuate a very pretty window, and draw attention to a spectacular view.

Doors

An architectural-patterned wallpaper border can be just the thing to offset a door in an entryway. Paint bedroom doors a bright color and apply a wallpaper border around the outside of the wall as a trim.

Architectural Details

Use borders to create architectural interest where none exists. I find wallpaper borders the best invention for basically lazy do-it-your-selfers. The project is simple and small enough to finish in a weekend and you get the impact  of having wallpapered the entire room. A wallpaper border can actually change a room from plain to interesting in a few hours.

Furniture

FAMILY HEIRLOOMS: A REASON FOR KEEPING OUTMODED THINGS

A family get-together is a time when many family members share childhood memories. If grandparents have passed away, sometimes their presence is felt just as if they were still there. Often their possessions reside in various houses owned by those nearest and dearest to them. These items, familiar to everyone in the family, might spark memories of different times spent together.

Shared Memories

Several years after my husband's grandmother passed away, we were visiting the home of one of his cousins. When my husband, Jon, walked into the dining room, he came face-to-face with the breakfront that once belonged to his grandmother. As a child he saw this piece of furniture daily in her house. It was just a large, old mahogany breakfront of no particular value or interest. But seeing it now, third-generation recycled, it had a different meaning, and made him instantly aware of the continuity between the generations of his family. All around there were other signs including a candy dish that sat in the same spot on his grandmother's coffee table, then on his mother's table, always filled with M&M candies.

When a family member dies, the relatives often get rid of the things that seem to have no particular value and are out of fashion. But sometimes an old, dark, mahogany breakfront can look surprisingly up-to-date in a modern environment—and can represent traditions and memories worth far more than the item itself. One of my most cherished family items is a chipped blue bowl that my grandmother always used to fill with blueberries but that I now use to hold fresh-picked strawberries. I once dropped the bowl and it broke in half. We glued it together and it stuck. I love that bowl more than any other I own.

More Than Monetary Value

Familiar things often have more value than we realize. They represent a continuation of a relationship. Those we love who are no longer with us may not physically be there to share, for example, in the celebration of a grandchild's marriage, but they would be quite happy to know their presence will always be felt. When we're faced with the problem of getting rid of old things from our ancestors, we might just make room for them if we consider the value of memories.

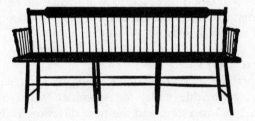

THE BEST OUTDOOR FURNITURE

Garden furniture is changing. No longer do we have to make do with unstylish chairs and tables made of molded resin or fiberglass. Good-looking furniture is now available in a wide variety of colors, made from attractive materials in all different price ranges.

Indoors and Out

Most garden and poolside furniture made today can easily work indoors as well as outdoors. For example, the selection of pieces by Brown Jordan is so extensive it would be hard to find anything to rival it. Whether you want aluminum, wrought iron, resin, or wood, whether your style is old world or contemporary, you'll find it in their extensive line of furniture. When buying outdoor furniture, buy it to last. Good pieces are a worthwhile investment, and it's easy enough to change the cushions or pillows when you want change from season to season.

Hard and Soft

I like to combine different textures, using wicker chairs with a wrought iron or marble table, for example. When everything matches it isn't as interesting and the new direction in decorating is mix and match. A well-proportioned wrought-iron garden table is sturdy and practical for indoor use and will look great between a floral print sofa and chairs.

The New Wicker

This new furniture is made by weaving resin over an aluminum frame so it won't fade, crack, or peel. It looks like old-time wicker but is virtually maintenance free. Most of the pieces from Brown Jordan, including chairs, chaises, ottomans, rockers, settees, and tables, are well designed for comfort. They are lightweight and rustproof and perfectly at home in any living room, indoors or out.

Dress Up Plastic Chairs

Of course if you can't afford really great outdoor furniture, dress up the $10 plastic resin chairs and inexpensive plastic molded tables you find in all home centers and even supermarkets. It's easy to do. Buy the separate seat cushions that are covered with woven plastic material and cover them with pretty fabric. I often just slip a pillow case over them and stitch across the end. Or you can attach ribbons evenly spaced across the open edge for tying. Use one or two tablecloths on the table. If using two, choose a solid color for the bottom cloth, and place a smaller, printed cloth on top. If the table is round, use a square tea tablecloth on top.

Colorful Additions

Add colorful occasional tables and planters around the patio. If you find a small table at a yard sale, for example, it's easy to weather-proof it for outdoor use with a coat of exterior weather-proofing stain or outdoor paint. First sand the original finish off the table, then apply the new finish. This is an easy and fun weekend project. Add a stencil design if desired by using outdoor paint for the stencils as well. Or use acrylic paint for the stencil and then give the piece a coat of clear varnish.

Make One Good Piece Count

If you can afford to buy only one really good piece of outdoor furniture, buy one that will do the most for you. For example, if you love to lie in the sun, choose a wonderful chaise that will give you extreme comfort every time you use it. This might be Brown Jordan's mission teak chaise, which easily adjusts to different positions and ages to a magnificent soft silver gray patina. You can use any other furniture with it. Or, if modern isn't your style, you might choose a wicker chaise made by the Lloyd Flanders company. These pieces are designed just as the original 1920s version but the material used today is weather resistant and more sturdy. However, the look is pure Gatsby luxurious. Stretch out in old-fashioned comfort and you'll feel instantly pampered.

A small loveseat is another great piece for the patio or porch. Whether it's made of wicker, wrought iron, or teak, just add plump cushions and you almost don't need anything else. Add a small table to hold a summer drink and you've got a look. Then you can use a few occasional chairs of less importance until you can afford better pieces.

Umbrella Tables

I think every outdoor living space needs an umbrella table. It almost creates a room all by itself. Once you've added an umbrella over an eating area, that space is instantly set apart as an entity. The umbrella should never be smaller than the table. It should always cover the entire tabletop to get maximum protection from the sun. And it looks better. I prefer the market umbrellas in natural and canvas and Hunter green. There are expensive versions and inexpensive copies. Actually some of the newer and less expensive ones are made of acrylic to look like canvas with the advantage of repelling water and resisting fading and mildew. But they look great with a light wood frame and brass fittings. The originals are more sturdy, of course, but I'm not sure there's any discernible difference in the look. You decide. For a more practical choice, the most common umbrellas are made from outdoor plastic resin. They're easy to clean with detergent and water and seem to last forever.

PAINTED FURNITURE

Unfinished or ready-to-finish furniture has come a long way and is still a great buy. The better-designed pieces, some influenced by Shaker style, blend perfectly with any other style of furniture. It's fun, easy, and especially satisfying to paint furniture because the transformation is instant. Anyone can apply paint without intimidation and now you can use paint creatively to achieve different styles. When you introduce painted furniture into a room with a few antiques or better pieces, it is instantly elevated. On the other hand, a room full of painted furniture can make a nice statement.

Accent on Style

The Rust-Oleum Company has come out with a twenty-page full-color booklet of color-coordinated decorating ideas using their new line of paint colors called American Accents™. The paints come in spray cans as well as easy-to-clean-up latex quarts and half pints. When you purchase any two sprays you can get the booklet free from American Accents Consumer Promotion, P.O. Box 8994, Clinton, IA 52736-8994.

For a Garden Room

Combine paint colors like summer squash, wildflower blue, leafy green, and blossom white. A garden room will look fresh and bright before you add even one plant when you paint different furniture pieces in summer colors like cinnamon, raspberry, light sage, and Indian spice. Pull together different styles, like wicker and wood, by giving them the same color treatment. Then use a second color for the accessories. Paint a bunch of clay or plastic flower pots in bright colors and group them on the floor or along a windowsill.

Tapestry Colors

Deep colors are nice in the bedroom and it's easy to create the look of built-ins with unpainted furniture. Choose low bureaus and place them end to end from one wall to the other. If they don't match exactly you can fill in one end with a false front made from a piece of wood. Or, have your lumberyard cut one long pine board to fit across the top of all bureaus so it fits between the walls even though there's a space between the bureau and the wall at each end. If the pine top butts between the walls it will give the bureaus the built-in look. Then do a creative paint job to tie them together. For example, you might choose hunt club green, claret wine, or midnight blue. For an interesting detail, paint all bureaus one color and then add a nutmeg or other light contrasting color to the door trim or knobs.

Primary Colors

Use primary colors on simple furniture in a child's room. For example, paint a rocker brilliant yellow, the bed frame berry red, and the bureau or toy box ocean blue. Then choose one of the colors for all the wood molding trim and another for the doors. You might even like to paint the inside of the closet bright yellow.

Classic Colors

For a dining room or den, use subtle old-world colors like taupe and colonial red along with hunt club or moss green. Paint the tabletop a lighter color than the legs. You might use maple sugar on the top with java brown on the legs. Then stencil a leafy vine border around the top with one of the green colors. Use this accent color to paint the dining chairs. Make seat cushions from a coordinating fabric.

Accessories

Paint raw wood boxes, window trims, wrought iron plant stands, and bookshelves for spots of bright color where needed. Imagine a room in rather subdued shades with just a few bright accents that work well together. The colors of nature are particularly nice to introduce into any color scheme.

 **WICKER**

We think of wicker furniture primarily for use on the porch or in a sunroom because of its light and airy quality. Good-quality antique American-made wicker has always been sought after by collectors and interior designers for use throughout the house. Because of their light weight, wicker pieces that are used indoors are often carried outside at the first hint of spring for sitting in the sun. Because they resist weather they are often used on decks and patios.

Wicker is the ideal furniture for summer homes. It evokes a feeling of nostalgia and casual informality. It has style and charm and it's easy to maintain. While you may not be able to find or afford a real antique, there are many wicker pieces to be found at flea markets, yard sales, and seconds shops. And of course there are reproductions, some better than others, depending on the price. For more information you might check out *Wicker Furniture: A Guide for Restoring and Collecting*, by Richard Saunders (New York: Crown Publishing Group, 1990). Here are some things to look for when buying wicker:

1. The framework shouldn't be rickety.
2. If there is any damage, be sure you know where you can get it repaired before buying it.
3. Sit in a chair or a sofa before buying. If it's uncomfortable, forget it.
4. If the paint is peeling you'll have to remove the old before recoating. Ask yourself how much work you're willing to put into the piece.
5. If it's a real beauty; if you love the piece; if it's in your price range; if it's not altogether perfect but not falling apart, and as long as you can use it, not just look at it; buy it.
6. If the seat is gone pass it by, unless you know how to recane or reweave or know someone who can do it for you.
7. If the furniture has its original finish (natural with no shellac or paint) buy it but don't do a thing to it.
8. If it's a real bargain, but needs a lot of work, in the end it may not turn out to be such a bargain; so don't buy it.

Now some advice for maintaining wicker:

1. Most wicker can be cleaned with soap and water.
2. To remove dust, just vacuum.
3. If your chair or sofa creaks when you sit on it, it's probably dried out. Take it outside, soak it with a hose and let it dry in the fresh air before taking it back inside.
4. Some dealers recommend going over your wicker piece with linseed oil. Just rub over all areas with a clean cloth. This will restore it.
5. If paint is peeling from your wicker, scrape off loose paint, clean the piece, and then apply a thin coat of spray paint. Let dry and

apply a thin coat of spray paint. Let dry and apply a second coat if needed.

Decorating with Wicker

Aside from porches, sunrooms, and summer cottages, wicker can be extremely versatile and adds romance and charm to any room. Here are some suggestions:

1. A chaise in the bedroom can be both pretty and practical. Pile it with lace pillows, drape a pastel mohair throw over the end, and you have an inviting corner for curling up with a book.
2. Add a Victorian wicker piece such as a writing table or a chair in the corner of a living room. The delicate pieces will be a welcome relief from overstuffed sofas and chairs.
3. A wicker coffee table balances well with a cushioned sofa.
4. Try placing a small wicker side table and chair on a stair landing or in a guest bedroom. Outfit the table with an elegant picture book, a lamp, and a small vase of cut flowers. You might even put a linen runner or teacloth on the table for a fresh, summery feeling.
5. An antique wicker sideboard would be functional and attractive in a dining room.
6. A graceful rocking chair doesn't always belong on the front porch. Consider this in a baby's room or a den where you might also have a deacon's bench or soft furnishings. Wicker rockers can be incredibly comfortable.
7. A classic white open weave rocker lightens and brightens a dark room. Add a white throw and a needlepoint pillow.
8. A wicker étagère or corner shelf is perfect for holding towels and necessities in the bathroom, and is much more elegant and lovely than other materials.
9. A tea table might lend an air of old-fashioned gentility to a living room. If you can find the perfect wicker chairs to go with it, all the better. Otherwise, delicate cane chairs with floral cushions would be a nice complement.
10. Accessories like magazine and book holders, washstands,

cribs, carriages and cradles, music stands, plant stands, vanities, sewing baskets, bric-a-brac stands, and bird cages are often used for purposes other than originally intended. Look for these as well as mirrors, headboards, bed trays, lamps, footstools, umbrella stands, and room screens to add character to your home.

BUYING OLD FURNITURE AND ACCESSORIES

I'm no expert on buying antique furniture, but I have many friends who are in the business and are always willing to share information. My inexperience, however, has never stopped me from going to auctions, flea markets, and yard sales because I'm forever in search of a bargain. Since I never pay a lot of money for an item I can only hope that, one day, one of my expert friends will exclaim over the terrific find I uncovered. In the meantime I buy only what I love or what I think has potential if redone with a new finish. Here are some tips I've gathered for those of you who love to forage for treasures among the old:

1. If a chair is rickety, forget it. If it has a missing seat it's easily repairable.
2. Dishes with chips and cracks aren't worth having. Eventually your china cabinet will look like Goodwill.
3. If you find an old quilt you love, but it needs repairing, be sure you can do the repairs. It's hard to get a quilt repaired.

4. If you find something you love and the price is right, don't hesitate; you'll always find a place for it.

5. Frames without glass are easy to repair. Almost any hardware store cuts glass to order and it's not expensive.

6. Buy the best you can afford of a particular item. You can always trade up as you can afford to. Often the first purchase in a collection isn't the last.

7. If you're looking for really good items, get a good, up-to-date guide book so you know what to look for.

8. When buying old furniture, I've found it particularly hard to fix drawers that don't fit right, and eventually it drives me crazy when the drawers don't glide in and out. I'm not talking about oiling, I'm referring to ill-fitting drawers that need rebuilding. Know your limitations when it comes to repairing.

9. Any finish can be removed. There are specific products in the stores that will take off shellac, varnish, paint, or wax. If the lines and size are appealing and you want to refinish, don't hesitate. These projects are usually fun and the piece will become a focal point in your room. More interesting than something new.

10. Anything silver is hot right now. But check the markings somewhere on the piece to be sure it's sterling and not plated. And even if you don't know prices, decide what something is worth to you. If it's within your price range and you like it, get it. Silver can't be too ornate. Even if your taste runs to contemporary in home furnishings, ornate silverware goes with everything. My mother told me that years ago when I poo-pooed the idea of picking out a fancy silverware pattern for my wedding gifts. Every time I entertain I get compliments on my place settings and will always be grateful for her advice.

FAST FAUX FINISHES

Faux finishes used to require a certain amount of talent in order to mix the chemicals needed for each technique and to apply them artfully to walls or furniture. Many companies have developed products to make it possible for anyone to create beautiful sponging, glazing, marbleizing, and combining effects without prior knowledge. These faux finishes are perfect for turning the most ordinary ugly items into interesting accessories. The materials are available in all home centers and hardware stores, and the ones I've had success using are from the Formby's Decorative Touches line.

Faux Finished Planters

I've been collecting containers to turn into planters. So far, my collection includes a few plastic urn-shaped cups, a milk-white lamp globe, tall plastic drinking glasses, a salad bowl, a plastic urn on a pedestal, a plastic tissue holder (turned upside-down for my use), and a set of kitchen canisters. Working with faux finishes that come in spray cans I've been able to make some of them look as if they 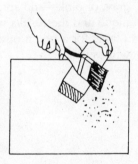 were made of granite in gray, white, and pink mauve. Some have been marbleized and others given an iridescent finish in pale peach, pink, lavender, green, and blue.

Peppery Candleholders

On a trip to the Salvation Army, I was determined to find chunky wooden candlesticks, but instead found a set of fat wooden salt and pepper shakers with peeling green paint. I removed the stopper from each, sanded them lightly, turned them upside down, sprayed them with granite, and inserted a candle into the hole. They are perfect!

Faking It!

These faux finishes that you spray onto metal, wood, or plastic are good for picture frames, too. Gather a few different sizes together and spray each with a different finish. It's amazingly simple, and the more you do, the more you'll like the results. Don't misunderstand, I would not use these products on a piece of fine furniture, convincing myself that I was creating a finish that resembled real marble. However, for recycling odds and ends that you have in your kitchen drawer, attic, or basement, the transformation is incredible.

Formica No More

If you have an old Formica table that's outdated, don't get rid of it. Marbelize. If the top is chipped, first fill in the gouges with a wood putty. Let it dry and sand smooth. It takes only minutes. Then choose the color marble you want—green, black, white, gray, or pink—and spray it on. It's the perfect project for this technique and the results will please you. This is a good way to finish a table for a porch or a rental home where you might like a bit of whimsy.

Fabric

DECORATING WITH FABRIC

I was at the opening of a quilt show and someone asked me if I thought the craft of quilting was still as popular as in its heyday. Ever since quilting really caught on in the early 1980s it has held its own as the most popular of the needle arts and probably of all crafts. In fact there are so many quilting classes, expos, and quilt exhibits all over the country that one could spend an entire year in the world of quilts, quiltmaking, and quilters.

Why Is Quilting So Popular?

It's easy to make a quilt. It's useful and incredibly rewarding. But more than that, I think it's an excuse to buy fabric. Everyone loves fabric. Ask any woman who sews and she'll tell you she can't resist a fabric shop, even when her sewing basket is already brimming with remnants. A fabric

shop is a place that brings out the creativity in anyone who sews. All those colors, patterns, and textures! I have friends who collect fabric for the imagined and not-yet-dreamed-up projects they intend to do in the near future. Some get done, others are "still evolving." All it takes is an interesting project, a great design, or a need for a soft furnishing to move a fabric lover into action. And there is no greater incentive than decorating our homes.

Satisfying the Creative Urge

Today, nobody crafts just to fill time. We have acquired an over-whelming interest in having nicely decorated homes and, for those who love to sew and love collecting fabrics, there is no better way to satisfy the creative urge.

Making simple projects, such as covering an old ottoman with a country blue-and-white Laura Ashley plaid, or using vintage fabric to create an elegant pillow, doesn't require a lot of previous sewing knowledge. And with time being a factor, even those who have been sewing for a lifetime don't want to make things that take a long time. However, the design and the end result should look nothing less than sensational. And this is one of the reasons quilting is so popular. The traditional designs are timeless. With new fabrics, you can take an early classic pattern such as a star or log cabin, and create a quilt that is suited to your own color scheme.

It's Sew Easy

Anyone who owns a sewing machine can make basic home accessories. They might include a pillow or placemats or a lovely wall hanging. If the motivation for making a project is to save money, fabric is quite inexpensive. You have the added advantage of being able to buy a small amount of a very expensive fabric to make an elegant pillow, for example, trim it with silk braid, and end up with an accessory that is worth several times what the material cost.

Affordable Chic

Many people sew for the satisfaction of making something themselves, or to have something that is unique. Sewing soft furnishings is satisfying because the end result is useful. A quilt is the perfect example of a project that fulfills our need to relieve stress; to have an ongoing activity that ends up with a practical item that contributes to the look of your home as well as your emotional well-being.

Are You a Fabric-holic?

A friend of mine admits to being a "fabric-holic." Collecting fabric can become addictive. If you've never gone into a fabric shop, even if you've never sewed a project in your life, take a peek. You won't be able to resist. During the holidays you'll find velvets, tapestries, brocade, taffeta, satin, moire, and of course all those cotton prints and colors. What fabric is best for quiltmaking? Most quilters will use only 100 percent cotton, but others concede to a blend of cotton and polyester because it doesn't wrinkle, shrink, or bleed. All cotton fabric should be washed before it is cut or sewn.

Start Small

If you're tempted to make a quilt, start small. A baby quilt is a terrific project, a great gift, and won't take long to complete. A small wall quilt is another good project. And if you really get carried away at the fabric shop, take a look at the many books on soft furnishings. You'll be inspired to make something, even if it's nothing larger than a curtain tieback.

 # SLIPCOVER TIPS

The other day I went in search of a good upholsterer to make slipcovers for my loveseat and two chairs. It wasn't difficult to find someone, but the cost would be about what I might pay for new furniture—without the fabric. I decided to see if I could do it myself.

Fabric: What Works Best

Weight is important. Too heavy is hard to sew and too light is not durable for the long haul. Medium weight is recommended, and I especially like ticking material and tapestry. Linen and cotton/polyester blends are practical for everyday wear. Plan to buy extra and prewash it for shrinkage before cutting out the pieces. Or have it cleaned.

Pattern Choices

Solid fabrics or those with an overall pattern are the easiest to cut and match. Fabrics with a large repeat pattern or a stripe, for example, require more yardage and more expertise. But if you want to add character to a room, choose the fabric that will do this for you. Love the fabric you choose because a slipcovered sofa is a lot of work, takes a lot of fabric, and is often the dominant object in the room. If the furniture underneath the slipcover is in good condition, think of using the slipcover in the alternate season and choose the colors, fabric, and pattern accordingly.

Estimating Amount of Fabric

Most upholstery fabric comes 52 inches wide. Measure all sides of the furniture to be covered, as well as front, back, and sides of the cushions. It's always a good idea to add a little extra for error and, don't forget, if you're matching patterns you will need quite a bit more. Consult with the person selling you the fabric to determine how much a standard-size chair or sofa usually takes. She or he will know from experience and be able to advise you.

Details That Matter

Pay attention to the things that add a finishing touch, such as the piping, buttons and bows, and other trimmings. You might like to have a scalloped edge on a dining chair cover or a contrasting piping for an outline defining the shape. A blue-and-white plaid piping, for example, would be attractive on a country sofa slipcovered in blue-and-white stripes.

Mix and Match

Combining patterns can create interest when everything is the same color. For example, if you choose a monochromatic scheme, use a solid-textured ivory fabric on the sofa arms, back, and cushions and a beige-and-eggshell stripe for the skirt. Or combine geometric prints with solids in shades of the same color.

How to Do It

I seem to fall under the "jump-in-with-both-feet-first" school of do-it-yourselfers as opposed to those who read, study, and then buy a step-by-step pattern. You can approach this project in either way. For the first, I recommend making pattern pieces from Kraft paper for each section of the furniture that will be covered. Next, cut these pieces from muslin and baste them together in order to adjust and get it right before actually cutting out the more expensive fabric. If you want, you can use the muslin slipcover as a lining to reinforce the finished project.

For the more precise among you, there are many patterns available for all different size and style furnishings. Simplicity and Butterick pattern books, for example, are available in fabric stores and have sections on home decorating with a variety of patterns from which to choose. They will help you calculate the amount of fabric needed.

Ottoman Slipcover

I found a terrific square ottoman at a yard sale. The shape was wonderful. But it was made of beige vinyl, cracked here and there, and not very pretty, or practical. The size and shape were great, but it needed a fabric slipcover to be acceptable for my family room. This is probably one of the easiest items to slipcover.

Measuring

Measure length and width of the top surface. Add an extra 1/2 inch to all sides for seam allowance and cut out the top. Next, measure the height and add 1 inch for seams. Then measure around the perimeter and add 6 inches. Cut out this band of fabric. If you don't have enough width to do this in one piece, cut two and stitch together to make a long enough strip. Use the perimeter measurement plus 4 inches to cut a strip of fabric 2 inches wide for the piping between the top and sides.

Stitching It Up

Place cording in the center of the wrong side of the fabric strip to make the piping. Match raw edges of the fabric, encasing the cording between, and stitch as close to the cording as possible. Then, beginning and ending 1 inch short of each end, sew the piping to the front edge of the ottoman top fabric. With right sides facing, stitch the wide, side fabric band to the piping. Fit this over the ottoman. Fold the seam edges to the inside and slipstitch the opening to finish. Pull the bottom, raw edge of the fabric tightly to the underside and staple in place.

 # PILLOWS

I love to make pillows. Not the kind you sleep on, but decorative throw pillows that can change the look of a room in an instant. I buy one or two yards of several fabrics that appeal to me and then try to come up with creative ways to combine them. Lately I'm down on ruffles and elaborate braids, tassels, and trims. Decorating is taking a turn for the simpler, and more basic classic looks are in. When making pillow covers, I like a crisp, finished treatment of matching or contrasting piping. If you have small remnants of fabric you'd like to use up, cut them into squares and create your own patchwork cover. Nine alternating squares of 6 inches each makes a nice size. Remember to cut each square 6¹/₂ inches for seam allowance. This is a nice simple winter project.

Pillow Sizes

If you make several pillows you'll want to combine different sizes. There is a size for every situation. For example, pillows on a porch sofa or bench should be on the large size—22 to 24 inches. Pillows on a sofa are usually 14, 16, and 18 inches. A 20-inch square is nice if you use only one on each side of the sofa, or for leaning against in bed behind your sleep pillow.

Filling

Some pillows should be filled so they are firmer than others, depending on use. They can be filled with pillow forms so they are quite firm, or with loose Polyfil™ stuffing if this is what you prefer. Pillows that go along the back of a bench on a deck might be firmer than those used under your head while lying on a chaise longue or thrown in a wicker chair. The Fairfield Corporation makes a pillow form called "Soft Touch" that feels like down but is actually Polyfil™, which keeps the cost down. It comes in all sizes.

Fabrics

Outdoor pillows should be covered with weather-resistant fabric that is sturdier than fabric used to cover indoor pillows. The fabric you choose should relate to the fabric already on the furniture or in the room. If you use a solid color for the largest pillow, make the smaller ones in matching color prints. Then you can use the print for the piping around the solid pillow. Also consider combining prints with checks and plaids. Or choose a color scheme and pick different fabrics in the same colors. I once made a bunch of pillows for my daughter's living room. The sofa was white and we combined blue and white stripes, checks, and polka dots, making a checked pillow with a polka-dot ruffle, for example. It worked quite well.

How to Do It

1. Cut two squares 1/2-inch larger than the size desired (this is the seam allowance). Cut 1 to 1 1/2-inch strips of piping fabric long enough to outline the pillow, plus an extra inch. Cording comes in various sizes. Use a fatter one for a casual look, a thinner one for a more formal finish.

2. Place the piping cord in the center of the wrong side of the fabric strip and wrap the fabric around it so the raw edges of the fabric meet. Use a zipper foot on the sewing machine and stitch as close to the encased cording as possible.

3. With the raw edges of the piping fabric aligned with the raw edges of the front of the pillow fabric, pin all around. Snip into the seam allowance at each corner for ease of turning. Stitch all around. When you get to where the ends meet, overlap the fabric from one end to the other to create a continuous piece.

4. With right sides facing, pin the back piece of pillow fabric to the front with the piping between. Stitch as close to the piping as possible around 3 sides and 4 corners.

5. Clip the corners and trim the seam allowance. Turn right side out and press. Press the open raw edges to the inside. Slipstitch the opening closed or insert a zipper.

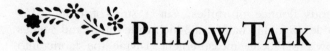# PILLOW TALK

Really smashing pillows made from interesting fabrics and edged with finishing details will make a blah sofa or chair more interesting. Lace pillows add romance to the bedroom. Ready-made pillows come in all sizes, shapes, and fabrics. But it's easy to make your own. In this way you can use sumptuous fabrics and special trimmings without spending a fortune.

Vintage

I love the look of vintage fabric. Old faded tapestries, silk, linen, and velvet exude an air of comfortable familiarity. Needlepoint pillows also have the look of antique elegance. Sometimes you can find a needlepoint remnant newly made to represent the past. Add a velvet backing and gold braid for the piping and you have a dynamite focal point in your room.

Contemporary

Heavy textured cottons and linens are quite exquisite when teamed with touches of gold. Gold cording, an appliqué medallion, antique beads or buttons, corner tassels, and silk braid are a few of the finishing touches you can use to dress up a damask fabric pillow.

Country Casual

When it comes to country pillows, the variety of fabrics and styles is limitless. Homespun is a plaid fabric that is finished on both sides. It comes in white with red, blue, yellow, green, and navy. It works with everything. And then there are the calicos and all sorts of prints. Mix and match the fabric and the piping and create interesting finishing touches like ruffles, buttons, and ties.

Finishing Touches

1. A generous flounce of ruffles: Cut a strip of fabric 6½-inches wide (to fold in half for a 3-inch wide ruffle) and 3 times the pillow's perimeter measurement. Divide the fabric into fourths and mark with a pin. With right sides facing and raw edges aligned, pin each marked spot to the corner of the top pillow fabric. Gather and pin the ruffle fabric between corners all around. Then stitch. Place the backing piece facedown on the front of the pillow and stitch around on top of the first stitches. Leave one side open for turning. Turn to right side, press, stuff, and slipstitch opening closed.
2. Button ends: Make a pillowcase and hem the open end with an extra 2 inches of fabric. Add four evenly spaced buttons to one side and make corresponding buttonholes on the opposite hem.
3. Stitch a square pillow cover with an extra 2½-inch flange all around. Line the flange with a contrasting fabric for interest. The center of the back will need an overlapping flap or zipper for inserting the pillow.
4. Fabric ties: Add fabric ties evenly spaced along the top open edge of a pillow cover. Tie with bows. If the pillow form isn't hidden, insert a pretty piece of fabric over the pillow end inside the slipcover.

Mix and Match

If you buy a fabric of the same print in different colorways you can easily mix and match for an interesting grouping of pillows. For example, I recently bought striped fabric in white with blue, rose, and aqua. The colors all work together because they're of the same value, having come from the same line of prints. It's hard to mix fabrics printed by different manufacturers. The pillows are oversized and 24 inches square, for the back of a daybed. I interchanged the fabrics for the piping on each pillow. The pink-and-white-striped pillow is edged with green-and-white piping, the green-striped pillow and the blue-striped pillows are edged with pink and white. You can do this with different prints and patterns as well. Or cut up squares of fabrics that look good together and make a piece of patchwork for a pillow top.

A Little Goes a Long Way

I'm a bit extravagant when it comes to buying fabric for pillows because it doesn't take much and the results are impressive out of all proportion to the cost. If a really nice tapestry pillow costs from $80 up, it's good to know you can make one for as little as $12. So, when buying fabric and trims to make pillows, keep this in mind. It takes less than a yard of fabric to make a large pillow, and only half a yard to make a pillow under 18 inches square.

IN LOVE WITH CHINTZ

Chintz is a fabric that I adore. We often see it used in very formal living rooms. Well-known decorator Mario Buatto has been dubbed the "Prince of Chintz" and if you're not familiar with his work, think roses. Lots and lots of floral-printed chintz is his trademark. In England, chintz was used only in country cottages and perhaps this is what originally influenced us. But the wonderful thing about chintz is that it can be formal or casual depending on how and where you use it.

Floral Chintz

Chintz has a wonderful rich sheen, yet the feel of 100 percent cotton. It holds its shape better than other similar fabrics. Chintz is to the new country style what calico used to be. It has a country feeling without looking passé. It can make a stuffy room look informal and at the same time dress up a very undressed room. Chintz comes in solid colors as well as prints and isn't expensive compared to other decorator fabrics. When I make curtains or drapes I always use plain white or cream-colored chintz. It's got a bit more character than plain cotton. Then I add very wide chintz tiebacks with a floral print on a white or cream background.

Regal Trims

It's fun to dress up chintz. For example, use the plain color for draperies or pillows and add elaborate trimmings. This dresses up the fabric without making it as formal as it would be if added to such fabrics as velvet and silk.

Color

There are certain color combinations that evoke country style. Blue-and-white checks have always been a favorite for summertime or vacation homes. But recently, adding yellow to this color scheme makes it more interesting. Pastel colors like pale pink combined with deep rose and brilliant green work well on either painted furniture or warm, rich woods. This is the new direction in country.

The Decorated Look

One of the great things about floral chintz is it makes a room look instantly decorated. You can add chintz fabric to plain windows, cover unsightly furniture, and any room will look stylish. You don't have to know much about decorating to work with it. Even mixing and matching prints seems to be okay. Plaids and stripes go well with florals, for example. Mix florals in similar colors and that works well. Or, do as I've done, and overdo a good thing. I have a particularly pretty cabbage rose print on my slipcovers. I've used it on the sofa and chairs as well as tiebacks and tablecloth and I never get tired of it. The furniture is getting a bit worn, but somehow the chintz fabric makes the room look fresh. It's not shabby. It's stylishly informal and getting to look as though the furniture has been in my family for a long time. If you have inherited furniture that isn't very good looking, consider chintz slipcovers. The fabric works wonders.

Room by
Room

KITCHEN SPACE: TIPS FOR GETTING ORGANIZED

If you're ready to make your kitchen function more smoothly, here's some advice from the folks at Builder's Square. Your local home center has all sorts of convenient items for making your kitchen more efficient.

Wasted Space

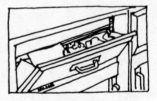

Turn wasted space into a small storage area by putting a tilt-out panel in the dead area between the sink and cabinet front. When most sinks are installed there's an area between the cabinet wall and the sink that's covered with a fake panel that doesn't open but gives the outside appearance of being a drawer. Simply remove the panel, cut the appropriate size opening if it doesn't already exist, attach a small plastic container to the panel and reconnect it with hinges at the bottom and an extending lock to hold it securely. This little addition comes in lengths from 11 3/4 to 14 3/4 inches by 2 inches wide and 3 3/4 inches deep. It's great for holding small cleaning tools.

Appliance Garage

This is a small housing unit that fits between the kitchen cabinet and countertop. You can install one in a corner to get more

space or place one on the countertop. The units are 12 inches deep
and, when placed on a standard 24-
inch countertop, that depth allows
for a 12-inch work area in front of
the appliance garage. When you're
through with the appliance, clean it
and tuck it back into the garage, out
of sight. The Builder's Square spe-

cialist estimates that two or three appliances will fit in a 24-inch-

wide garage, three appliances in one that's 27
inches, and three to four in a 30-inch unit. They
come in dozens of wood colors or you can paint
it to match your existing color.

Pull-Out Basket Drawers

These are the most useful home improve-
ments for kitchen efficiency. They are
installed on a set of rollers that pull the contents out of the cabinet for easy access. No
more reaching into the back of cabinets. If
you have an area that's several feet high, you
can install a flat roller drawer on the bottom
and a set of roller baskets half the distance to
the top of the space. These baskets are ideal
for storing potatoes, onions, apples, etc.

They're made of metal mesh covered with plastic and allow ample
air circulation.

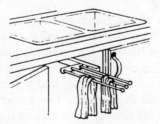

Space Savers

Several items can be attached under the cabinets over the countertop: A cutlery tray for knives and a cookbook holder, or a message center complete with notepad and clipboard are space savers that fold up out of sight.

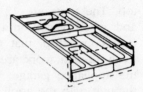

MAKING A SMALL LIVING ROOM SEEM LARGER

If you have a small room that feels cramped, there's no need to knock down walls to get a feeling of spaciousness. In fact there are all sorts of decorating tricks to solve this problem.

Grand Reflections

If the room is a rectangular shape and seems too narrow, arrange your furniture in a square, away from the walls. Then mirror one narrow wall to reflect the furniture arrangement. Mirrors visually expand any space and represent a simple solution to a cramped look.

All of a Piece

Use one color on all the furniture, rugs, and walls. To avoid a boring look, select different textures and shades of the same color. A natural tone would be best. For example, the furniture slipcovers or upholstery could be a textured linen, the floor could be covered in sisal or with an Oriental rug, and a faux finish paint treatment could be applied to the walls. Use a contrasting color, such as a darker shade of the natural, for all wood trim. Then add paintings or prints to the walls. One big painting in a small room has more impact than a small grouping.

Don't Overcrowd

Make every piece count. Choose a few good pieces with clean lines and take away clutter. One large piece can be the focal point of the room. It might be a sofa, an armoire, or two loveseats opposite a large coffee table.

Making It Homey

The above suggestions might make you think the room is too stark and not cozy enough. A homey feeling can be achieved easily with the use of earth tones, honey-colored woods, a soft textured blanket over the ottoman or sofa, and a pile of books on a table.

Combining Textures

I like to use formal textures with informal ones. For example, use a tapestry pillow on a leather sofa on a wood floor. Into this setting you might add a marble or glass table for a formal look, or a wood table for a less formal approach. Stripped pine furniture is always informal, giving any room a country feeling. Painted furniture is also less formal than furniture made from woods such as mahagony, cherry, or oak.

Arrangements

How you arrange your furniture makes a big difference. If you want to create seating for six in a small living room, for example, you might consider a comfortable cushy loveseat in place of a full-size sofa. Then add two medium-sized cushioned chairs. Two small occasional wooden chairs that are considerably smaller and fit on either side of a window or desk can be pulled over to be part of the intimate seating arrangement when needed.

TIPS FOR ODD-SHAPED LIVING ROOMS

Do you often wish that your living room was just a tiny bit larger? longer? squarer? This happens to me every time I have company. Don't despair. Fool the eye with these decorator tricks to make a small or odd-shaped rooms seem well proportioned.

1. Don't line the furniture against the wall in a long, rectangular-shaped room. Rather, create a conversational square in the center of the room.
2. Keep everything in the same color tone. Lots of colors and mixed patterns might be interesting, but they tend to make a room look busier and often smaller. A monochromatic color scheme makes a room look airier, cleaner, and larger.
3. Use a few large pieces rather than lots of small pieces of furniture. Make every one count.
4. Choose light wooden furniture and keep surfaces clear of knickknacks.
5. Lighting can be tricky. Play around with different lighting techniques to see what works best under different circumstances.
6. Window treatments should allow for the most amount of daylight and window exposure. Wooden blinds are currently in style and are good for adjusting light and privacy without covering more than the window opening. For a softer look, choose light fabric panels that can be drawn back on each side.

7. Wall-to-wall carpeting makes a room look larger than if you use area rugs, but I like exposed wooden floors. One large area carpet is more effective than small scatter rugs for a spacious look.

8. Sometimes space looks smaller than it actually is due to a lack of light. If a small remodeling job is in the budget, consider adding a window or removing part of the ceiling or taking down a wall to create a feeling of more space in a room. Maybe a skylight or converting a regular window into a bay window is the answer.

9. Boat builders know the true meaning of small and make every inch count. Think about how the cabin of a boat is planned out. It might inspire you to think about furniture that creates a feeling of built-ins.

10. For a minimal change that can affect the look of any room, a fresh coat of paint will do wonders. A soft white is probably the best choice for awakening a tired room. It's safe, but always up-to-the-minute and will accept any color you introduce. Don't make the mistake of thinking any other color will do what only a shade of white can do—and that is, make a room look larger

A Cottage Built for Two...or More!

Recently the *New York Times* Living section had an article about how and why houses continue to grow in size. The article also enumerated the advantages of living in smaller space. I rather like what Michael Walsh, a syndicated columnist has to say on the subject: "Excess square footage is the architectural equivalent of overeating, with all its overtones of nervous disorder." We complain that young people starting out can't afford to buy their own homes, but there is a conspiracy to keep building big. At the same

time families are shrinking and more single people are buying homes. According to a recent study by an arm of the National Association of Home Builders, 30 percent of the homes built last year had four bedrooms or more. In six years it is predicted that the average American home will be 2,500 square feet. Good living, however, is not related to square footage.

A Case for Intimacy

Small spaces represent intimacy and simplicity in living. Since it costs less to build a small house, you can be lavish with quality and details you might not be able to afford in a larger building. And you don't end up with a jumbo mortgage. Considering maintenance and upkeep and utilities, a small house is simply affordable.

More Praise for Small

It's challenging to make small spaces interesting and to understand that less space doesn't have to mean cramped space. In fact, a one-room cottage can be as delightful and efficient as any other home can be. Here are some tips for making an interior look larger than it is.

1. Never use dark paint or quaint furnishings. The walls and ceiling should be painted bright white, light gray, pale blue or green, or linen white.
2. Suggested fabrics might be large and airy floral prints combined with crisp, blue-and-white ticking for curtains and furniture. Tiny, overall prints make everything look smaller.
3. You might assume you'd find precious furniture in a small cottage, but instead you should carefully furnish with just a few large and comfortable pieces like an ample loveseat or sofa, an overstuffed armchair, and a more delicate woodframe chair arrangement around a coffee table. A mix of antique pieces with contemporary accessories and selected paintings will make a small home quite stylish.

4. Use shelves wherever possible, such as open shelves in the kitchen or a high shelf running around the room for books or displays.

5. Add window boxes outside windows so the flowers will be seen from indoors. A vase of fresh flowers is all that's needed on the coffee table.

6. Choose furniture that can do double duty. For example, a trunk might be useful as a side or coffee table and also holds bulky items like blankets.

7. A side table can double as a buffet, and, if it has a drawer, can be used for storing table linens.

8. A corner hutch is a good item for holding books and collectibles on the open shelves, with closed storage below.

9. A dry sink is useful as a bar with storage for glasses and bottles below.

10. If you buy regular dresser drawers of the same size and height to fit along one wall, you can create the look of built-in storage with a work or display space on top.

BATHROOM MAKEOVER

How many times do you feel you need more bathroom space? If you're like me, every morning is a reminder that the smallest room in the house really is. Builder's Square has some tips for bathroom makeovers that cost as little as $250.

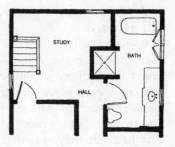

Wallpaper

Go for brightness with a new look provided by wallpaper and paint. They estimate wallpaper to cost $120 for an average-sized bathroom. This is a good way to give your room character. I once had a tiny powder room that didn't have a window. I chose a bold floral print (which might seem outrageously wrong, but it was great) and papered all the walls and ceiling to create a very lush environment. A jungle print is another great solution. Tiny rooms don't have to be papered in tiny prints.

Paint

For a less expensive redo, paint will cost about $50 with another $20 for brushes. Don't forget to paint your baseboards a contrasting but complementary color to match the new wallpaper or paint.

Lighting

If your lighting is inadequate, install a fluorescent light for about $50. Or keep the lighting fixture you have but change the standard switch on the wall to a rheostat to control the lighting. A new overhead light will modernize the room. A dark bathroom tends to appear dingy, no matter how clean it is. Add wall sconce lights to either side of the mirror.

Floor

Vinyl tile is very replaceable. Congoleum has an incredibly wide range of textures, colors, and styles and this is a good, inexpensive way to change the look of your bathroom. There are sheet vinyls and do-it-yourself tiles with sticky peel backs for easy installation. You can even get the look of marble in several colors for an elegant finish.

Windows

A single pleated shade over the window can make a big difference, but keep the color light. Hunter Douglas pleated shades called Duette honeycomb shades combine soft, seamless fabrics and crisp, even pleats in hundreds of colors. They come in sheer and semisheer for diffused light to semiopaque for filtered light. The opaque fabrics block the sun. Because they're durable and easy to clean, they're perfect for the bathroom.

Fixtures

A new towel rack, new towels, faucet handles, and electric switch plates on the wall are items that can easily be replaced to make your bathroom more modern and efficient. It isn't difficult to change faucet handles because most fixtures come in one piece. If you paint or wallpaper, cover the switch plate as well.

Bathroom Organizer

One of the last places to get organized has got to be the bathroom medicine cabinet. To the rescue comes the Medicine Cabinet Organizer insert, which is a unit made of recyclable polystyrene that fits into most standard medicine cabinets and creates up to 40 percent more usable storage space. It achieves this with an adjustable shelving system and special features that accommodate hard-to-store items like toothpaste, toothbrushes, razors, and ointments. The unit has a self-adhesive tape on the back to hold it firmly in place and it can be installed in minutes with no tools required. Now that's my kind of home project.

BATHROOM FIXTURES

Let's face it. Toilets aren't exactly glamorous items when it comes to interior design. If you're putting in a new bathroom, however, it's something you'll have to think about. And you'll be surprised at how many styles of toilets, sinks, and other fixtures there are to choose from. Taking a little time over this decision will be well worth the effort in the long run. After all, how many times does one change a toilet once it's installed?

European Style

A friend of mine who travels often to Europe was intrigued by European bathroom fixtures. When building her own home she duplicated some of the items with American-made products that had the essence of European styling. For a classic, yet contemporary, sophisticated and softly rounded look, there is a wonderful toilet design called "Cascade" by Mansfield. It flushes by pulling the handle up from the top of the rounded tank and comes in blue or gray. It actually saves on water and, if one could call a toilet cute, this best describes its design.

Fixtures Galore

When it comes to bathroom fixtures for tubs, sinks, and showers, the choices are mind-boggling. Faucets can change the entire look of the room. You can update an old bathroom by simply installing contemporary fixtures. If you aren't handy you will need a plumber to do this, but it's a very simple job for someone who knows what he or she is doing. Some people like an old-fashioned look in a brand new house. Whatever your choice you will find many more to choose from than you can imagine. Take the time to look at catalogs from various manufacturers because prices vary as much as the styles.

A GOOD NIGHT'S SLEEP

Every time the name Martha Stewart comes up it is quickly followed by someone saying, "Did you know she gets by on only three or four hours sleep a night?" Well, that explains it. I can't function on fewer than eight hours, so this means that Martha is ahead of me by four or five hours every single day. No wonder she can accomplish all that she does.

I think that many of us feel the effects of sleep deprivation. Anyone with children certainly does, and so do those facing the stresses of long commutes, long hours, and long lists of social and family obligations. Do the following questions strike a chord?

1. Have you been feeling grouchy lately and blaming it on the holidays?
2. After dinner do you begin to yawn and feel drowsy and blame it on the big meal you just ate?
3. Do you blame the stuffy air in the room for feeling sluggish?
4. Are you irritable and snappish?
5. Do you complain about anything and everything, lose energy and motivation?
6. Do you function best in mid morning and early evening, but most of the time can't perform at peak?

News Flash from the Better Sleep Council in Washington, D.C.

If you have one rotten night's sleep you can perform routine tasks, but you're not going to be especially creative. A second night's lost sleep and you can't even perform mundane chores.

Instant Face-Lift

One evening an old friend arrived on the island. He complimented me on looking especially good. "It must be because I spent most of the holiday weekend in bed catching up on my rest," I offered. "That's it," he said. "You look well rested." If that's all it takes to look like I'd had a face-lift, I'm all for increasing my sleep time. Sundays have always been a time to play catch-up with my work. Now I intend to use a few of those hours for getting "beauty rest." So that time-worn phrase didn't come from nowhere!

Did You Know?

1. Adults average 7.5 hours sleep a night.
2. Most of us get less sleep than we need. Surely the best gift one can give new parents is babysitting time so they can just close their eyes for two hours straight.

3. In a research study it was proven that if Americans had no time schedule whatsoever, they would sleep one more hour than they usually do.
4. If you or your grandparents get up around 4:00 A.M. and often doze off in the middle of the day, or while watching TV early in the evening, you are just part of a growing statistic. Over half of the 19 million people over sixty-five in this country experience insomnia and excessive daytime sleepiness. Sleep problems will increase as the population ages.
5. People are working more and resting less. In the last twenty years we have added a full month, or about 158 hours, to our annual work schedules. Where does the extra time come from? Usually the night.
6. Sleep deprivation has created a silent epidemic of daytime drowsiness.
7. Stress sabotages sleep. The more stressed you are, the more you can't sleep. And the more tired you are, the less capable you are of coping with stress, so you become even more stressed.

Getting More Sleep

So, okay, we admit it. We all could use more sleep. But how can we get it?

1. Napping may be what we're meant to do. The urge to rest in the afternoon is nearly universal, according to the study.
2. A normal dip in body temperature occurs about twelve hours after the midpoint of our nighttime sleep, which is just when we begin to feel drowsy.
3. Young children, college students, and retired people (those with schedules that allow siestas) nap most.
4. Taking a nap before what you suspect will be a restless night is more effective than taking a nap the day after a poor night's sleep. It's more difficult to make up for lost sleep than to prepare for it.
5. Ten-minute time-outs for relaxation exercises or meditation during the day will help anyone who feels he or she needs more rest.

Top Ten Tips for a Good Night's Sleep

1. Keep regular hours. To keep your biological clock in sync, get up at the same time, regardless of how much or how little you've slept.
2. Exercise regularly. This burns off tension. The ideal time to exercise is late afternoon or early evening.
3. Cut down on caffeine, chocolate, Chianti, and cheddar cheese.
4. Sleep on a good bed. A bed is not like a broken-in pair of running shoes. If you've had the same mattress for more than ten years, it's time for a replacement.
5. Six hours of good solid sleep is better than eight hours of light sleep. Limiting the time you spend in bed deepens sleep. I don't like this one because I truly love being in bed—reading, working, talking on the phone, or eating—and have been under the misguided idea that I am storing up rest. My adage is "If it feels good how can it be bad?"
6. Don't go to bed stuffed or starved.
7. Set aside worry or planning time before going to bed. A friend of mine says that when she wakes in the middle of the night worrying about trivial things, she forces herself to imagine what she'd buy if she could replace her entire wardrobe. This makes her fall asleep. Find something that works for you. I think about new ways to move my furniture around.
8. Establish a sleep ritual.
9. Keep the room at the right temperature for optimum comfort.
10. I work at perfecting my "bed style." This involves just the right softness of sheets. New ones are not nearly so good as those that have been washed a trillion times. In fact, old cotton sheets are really the best if not the prettiest. Several pillows in different stages of puffiness are required for different moods and position changes during the night. A down comforter that is lightweight but very cozy and warm is a must in the winter, a lighter one in the summer. Low lighting, night tables at just the right height, and a place for everything near and dear to you so that you don't have to get up for a single thing are also helpful.

IN THE DINING ROOM: SETTING A SENSATIONAL TABLE

Starting with Napkins

Giving a party personality can begin with napkins. They can be the basis for a table setting theme, or, for that matter, the theme for an entire party. Creative napkin folding is very much like the Oriental art of origami (folded paper designs). You can create fabulous napkin folds for holidays, birthdays, formal events, seasonal celebrations, and children's parties. Napkins provide the perfect way to create a mood, establish a theme, add a splash of color, and coordinate your table setting. This is an easy way to express creativity.

Create a Theme with Color

When choosing your theme, select napkins in the color and pattern that reflect the design. For example, to create roses, you might use pink or red solid or printed fabric. To make a boat shape, choose a blue-and-white pattern. For a children's party, a pinwheel napkin fold looks great with striped or polka-dotted napkins.

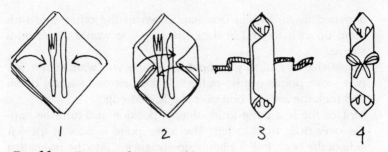

1   **2**   **3**   **4**

Buffet Brunch Bundle

Your guests will appreciate the convenience of having their silverware and napkin wrapped together. Napkins in fall colors might be good for a Labor Day brunch. Tie a napkin around a pot of chrysanthemums for table decoration. Cut a length of 18-inch satin ribbon for each napkin.

1. Fold a square napkin into quarters. Place napkin on the diagonal and center the silverware on it. Fold a small triangle in on each side corner.
2. Fold the napkin in thirds, enclosing the silverware, and tie a ribbon around the package.

Boating Party

Choose navy blue and white napkins for this party and add blue-and-white checked plates (paper or china). Use a buoy or floats as a centerpiece.

1. Fold the four corners of a square napkin to the center.
2. Bring the top point down to the bottom point without disturbing the already folded layers.
3. Fold the napkin in half from left to right.
4. Rotate the napkin slightly so the long edge of the triangle is at the bottom. You should have four folded edges at the bottom.

Separate them, two in one hand, two in the other, and turn them up in front and in back the way you would a cuff on a sleeve.

5. Adjust size of cuff to give boat the shape you want. There are two loose points on the right. Pull the first one slightly down and tuck the second one over the folded edge.

6. Replace the first point to its original position and turn the napkin over from right to left. The loose point is now at the left side of the boat. Pull it slightly up and tuck it into the layers that form the hull. Stand it up and insert a toothpick with a paper sail bearing each guest's name.

Bouquet of Roses for a Luncheon

Use pretty napkins arranged in a basket with sprigs of real flowers like baby's breath for your centerpiece.

1. Fold left edge of napkin over about 2½ inches.
2. Curl up the bottom edge and wrap hem edge once around your left index finger. Hold in place with middle finger.
3. Bring top edge down and up, winding the hem around three fingers. Bring top edge down and up again, winding hem end around four fingers.
4. Continue winding loosely until napkin is rolled up.
5. With right hand, tightly pinch napkin at the ends of your left fingers. Hold pinch firmly and remove left hand.
6. With both hands, continue to pinch napkin at the base of flower. Twist a stem under the flower by tightly pinching the napkin and twisting your hands in opposite directions as tightly as possible until you reach one-third down length of stem.

7. Find loose outside corner at bottom of stem end and gently pull at this corner, lifting it up until the tip reaches the flower to form the rose's leaf.
8. Tightly pinch base of leaf and twist until you reach bottom of stem. Insert into basket.

NURSERIES TO GROW ON

When my daughter had her first baby she furnished his nursery in soft pastels. The floor was carpeted in gray, the walls were painted soft yellow, and the crib was outfitted with pale aqua. She painted a rocking chair white and an unfinished dresser in pale yellow with white knobs. Shelves were filled with stuffed animals and she carried this theme to the walls with one of the 3M Decorator kits for putting up a peel-off border of dancing animals. Now that Tyler is two, he's ready for a bed and he wants cars on his walls. It's time for a change.

Bed Bargains

This is one item you don't have to spend a lot of money on. It's often easy to find old wooden bed frames at yard sales. Those made of maple, for example, are nice and sturdy if not so beautiful. But they're easy to paint in a bright color. Or, give it a coat of bright white (lead free) and add a stencil of blue-and-white checks around the sides.

Country Checks

Sheets are often less expensive than buying fabric by the yard. Choose blue-and-white gingham sheets, for example, and use one to make café curtains. Since a sheet is already hemmed, measure up from the bottom and cut the length needed to fit the window, adding enough fabric to stitch a channel to hold the curtain rod.

Stencil Wall Border

Using the same simple checkerboard theme, stencil a border around the wall just at the windowsill level. Once you have the checkerboard border you might want to add another illustration. For Tyler we added cars, but you might prefer balloons, tumbling clowns, sailboats, or teddy bears. Precut stencils can be found in art supply stores along with the acrylic paints and stencil brushes you'll need. Plan the placement of the stencil on the wall; in this case the cars were evenly spaced above the checkerboard border and each car is stenciled in a different primary color. When your child gets older it's easy to paint or paper the wall with a new color or pattern.

Storage Units

A two-year-old child wants his or her toys within easy reach, and you'll want storage that makes clean-up relatively simple at the end of the day. Large baskets are indispensible. An inexpensive low shelving unit of unfinished wood is easy to paint in bright colors. Each cubby holds different toys and books, and the top is the perfect height for a small child to stand at to run trains or trucks or play with a doll house. Everything in a toddler's room should be childproof and accessible. When possible keep the center of the room open for play.

HOME OFFICE

More and more people are working out of their homes, and if they aren't working at home full-time, they are certainly bringing work home from the office. Even if it's just having a workable space to keep household records, it's important to make this space just right for maximum efficiency.

Comfort, Looks, Function

If your space is comfortable and good looking you will gravitate to it and the work you do there will be rewarding. Yes, even paying bills! A home office doesn't have to look industrial. You can combine interesting objects with high-tech equipment for a space that is good looking and functions well.

Finding Space

When her last child went off to college, a friend of mine converted her daughter's bedroom into her office. "I love this room," she said. "I spend so much time here. I love the way I've organized everything just for me." She used ordinary plastic milk crates on shelves for her files, which suited her needs just fine. Everyday she feels more and more comfortable in this space as she perfects it. If you work at home you might consider the look and function of your area. Make it work best, but also think about making it look better. Think about what it needs and how you can best achieve it.

Consider Colors

For a country look combine the old and the new with colors used in imaginative ways. The interplay of worn paint colors on antique accessories like boxes, with newly painted furniture can be smashing. Chairs don't have to be secretarial, but should be comfortable. Consider a sofa or day bed in the office and cover it with fabric that reflects the same colors in the rest of the room.

Wall Treatment

A soft spatter-painted, sponged, or ragged finish will add a handsome texture to the walls. This is a good background for hanging interesting artwork, prints, or maps. For a country look, consider hanging a small quilt.

Window Treatment

A simple tailored window treatment looks best in an office. You might consider fabric shades or mini blinds for easy adjustment of light and privacy. Shutters are also good looking and practical.

Arranging Shelves

The things on your shelves can be decorative and still functional. Arrange objects that you like so they look good together without looking too studied. A mix of early folk art with modern office equipment is an interesting way to integrate a home office with your interior design while still functioning with high-tech efficiency.

Storage

CLOSETS

Is your closet a mess? Mine is always neat as a pin—for two days of every year. One, when I put away my summer clothes on the very last day I possibly can get away with shorts and T-shirts, and another on the last day of cold weather. On those two days of the year I revel in how organized I can be before chaos takes over my life. So you can imagine my delight to discover that there's a certified storage specialist at Builder's Square with the answer to my prayers for 365 days of closet neatness. Becky Marak is like a closet ghostbuster who takes about a minute to give you a plan that will take only one day to implement.

At the Builder's Square "Idea Center" they have something called "One-Minute Storage Solutions" that pop out of a computer programmed to combat most storage problems with a design for the do-it-yourselfer. No, they don't send Becky to your house once a week to reorganize you, but they give you a plan so you can do it right once and for all.

Closet Plans

Most homes have standard clothes closets that are roughly 6 feet wide and 2 feet deep. A utility closet might be deeper—at least 3 feet—and wider—anywhere from 7 to 8 feet—especially if it holds a washer and dryer. So the computer holds closet plans for most home situations.

You Do the Prep Work

Most bedroom closets are simple affairs with a metal hanging rod and a wooden shelf above it running the full length of the closet. It's easy to strip the closet to its bare walls, and if you can handle a hammer, a level, a drill, a quarter-inch drill bit, and a tape measure, you're on your way to the ultimate in organizing everything in your life. Once you've accurately measured, take those measurements to the store and they design the space and cut all the shelves and hanging rods to specification. Then you go home with everything you need to put it together.

How It Works

Using a standard closet as a model, the space is divided into three vertical areas, each 2 feet wide, topped with a 6-foot wall-to-wall shelf suitable for wardrobe or extra bedding. The 2-foot vertical areas to the left and right are used for hanging clothes. One side is left unobstructed for longer clothing such as dresses or coats. The other side has a clothes hanger bar at the top of the closet, and a second clothes hanger bar midway to the floor. This double hanging space can be used for blouses, skirts, shirts, and suits

The area in the center is divided into two 2-foot, full-width linen and wardrobe shelves. The 2-foot area under them is divided into one section of three 1-foot-wide personal storage areas. Alongside it is a drawer system created from 1-foot-wide stacked wire baskets. The closet renovation is completed with a shoe rack accessory. The estimated cost is roughly $140 to turn a standard closet into a deluxe haven of organization.

Do It Yourself

If you don't have a Builder's Square near you, check your local home center for all the materials to custom-outfit your closet on your own. It's easy to do with the new rubber-covered wire shelves that can be cut to fit any space. Plan carefully before buying the materials. Measure each area and plan how you will organize shoes, shirts, pants, and long dresses before cutting each shelf and upright.

 # STORE IT ALL

There's always a way to find extra storage space if you get clever about it. All it takes is looking at what you have with fresh eyes.

In the Bathroom

Rather than hanging a shelf above the mirror or medicine cabinet, make a frame of storage cubbies around this area.

Hallway Clutter

Organize kids' outdoor gear with a high shelf and cubbies beneath it along a hallway wall. Add hooks for easy hanging of coats and hats just like they have in elementary and nursery schools. Add a bench underneath for sitting and putting on boots. In fact, choose a bench with a lift-up top so that you can store unsightly items inside.

Kitchen Clean-Up

Staple a row of fabric every twelve inches under the cabinets with the fabric between the staples hanging down slightly like a hammock. Use each cubby for storing items you reach for often.

Attach a wooden dowel along an empty wall space for drying dish towels or for holding cloth napkins within each reach.

Above Doorways

If you have space between the top of the door frame and ceiling, use it to hang a shelf from wall to wall. This is a good out-of-the-way area to store items you don't need often such as punch bowls and other items for holiday entertaining.

Create small cubbies down one side of a doorway where there is a small wall area. Use it for books and collectibles.

Under the Stairway

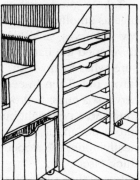

Use the space under stairways for graduated shelves. You might even be able to add a wider shelf below the storage shelves to create a desk area for at-home office work. Shelves can be anywhere from 8 to 12 inches deep. A desktop should be about 24 inches deep and 28 inches from the ground.

# BASIC CHANGES

From time to time we all need to make changes so our homes function better for our needs. Here are some ideas that might work for you.

Kitchen

Everyone needs a little private nook for taking care of home paperwork. If the space is bright and cheerful, and if you don't have to clear away dirty dishes each time you need to use it, you'll find it's much easier to pay bills and take care of household correspondence. Choose a table that will fit against a wall space. You can get an inexpensive unfinished table and paint it in the color of your choice or stain it with a wood color. Next select a comfortable chair in a contrasting or matching color. Use wicker baskets for filing and add attractive desktop accessories as well as a good-looking lamp (not an unused bedroom castoff). Hang shelves above the desk and add a bulletin board between the desktop and the shelves. This whole setup, when purchased from places like Pier 1 Imports or Crate 'N Barrel, will cost approximately $300.

Finding Space

Take a good look at your attic. Can it be used to your advantage as an office, playroom, or guest bedroom? Last year I did this. My attic was small, dark, and a mess. Over the years we had developed the habit of shoving anything up there that we weren't sure what to do with, had outgrown, or didn't want to keep or throw out. Then I needed an out-of-the-way office that could also serve as a guest bedroom when needed. With a great deal of planning and a very tight budget, I was able to convert unusable space into a delightful office with a half bath and two daybeds tucked neatly under the sloped roof, an area too low to be useful for anything else.

I used low, unfinished kitchen cabinets to create built-in storage under another area where the roof slopes down. The cabinets were 18 inches high, and you can use as many as needed to fill any space from wall to wall. Add a pine board to fit across the top of all of them to make it look like one unit. I painted the cabinet doors and stained the top in a wood finish. Add porcelain knobs and you have an inexpensive, good-looking wall of storage.

Closet

Change the way you use your closet and get organized. If you have an extra closet, use it as a laundry center. Outfit it with shelves and wicker storage baskets—rather than plastic bins—to keep everything separated. Or remove everything from a bedroom closet and start over with a plan and measurements. Draw out your ideal closet for storing everything more efficiently. You might use one of those closet systems with wire shelves that are available at home centers. Take your plan to the store so you buy exactly the elements you need.

Kids' Room

Make your child's bedroom or a family playroom carefree and fun. Use trunks for storing toys. Select a large, low table for all activities from coloring to setting up trains. For older kids' rooms or a family room, fold-up director's chairs are terrific. They don't take up lots of space, can be folded away when space

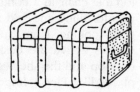

is needed, are inexpensive, and come with brightly colored washable canvas covers. For a practical window treatment, rice paper blinds are inexpensive and light. The cost for a sturdy table, two director chairs, a good size trunk, and window covering for three average-size windows would be about $500.

Organizing

 # PRIORITIES

"How was your summer?" is a common question right after Labor Day. Almost everyone I've spoken to has answered in the same way. "It was great. But now I have a lot of catching up to do." For those busy working, their personal lives need reorganizing. From my friends who freelance I've heard, "I didn't do much work all summer and now I have to run like crazy to get work." Getting organized in the fall seems to be of a major concern. Mothers with children in school make resolutions to organize busy schedules that tend to get out of hand as the school year progresses. "I'm determined to make lunches the night before." says one mother of two. And from another, "I'm going to get each child his and her own alarm clock so I'm not the one pulling them out of bed each morning." And so it goes. One mother with a senior in high school vows to do all the motherly things she wished she had time for the past. I remember each of my daughter's last year at home. I spent a lot of time making up for all my past neglects. I drove them crazy with my frantically inadequate attempts at making sure I had armed them with all the right "know-how" to carry forth into the world without me. Everything became equally important; baking cookies was right up there with lessons in morality.

But now, thankfully, my concerns are more mundane. I worry about my house. I ponder the earth-shaking dilemma of "to slip-cover, or not." Should I write about trends in furniture or lifestyle? It is so refreshingly liberating because a decision one way or the other is of no particular consequence.

What Comes First

Many of us have different areas of our homes that nag for attention. Every time my husband went into the basement last summer, he would come up muttering, "I have to organize and throw some things away." But it took until the week after Labor Day for the burst of energy for that particular project to kick in. Since we can't do everything at once we have to make priorities. Unfortunately maintenance comes before decorating. If the summer was particularly humid many of us ask, "Is that stain or mildew on the wall, or is there a water leak somewhere?" Take care of the things in order of importance and everything will get done.

Change of Seasons

If you live in an area of the country where weather changes with the season, you'll want to do outdoor maintenance while the weather is still nice. Cleaning up outdoor furniture, reassessing the garden, bringing things in, and finding places to put them come first. Once in a while I imagine it being easier to live where the climate never changes. I hate packing away off-season clothes because my closet is inadequate for two season's worth. But, in a way, the change of seasons gets us organized. Every seasonal

change is a chance to weed out and edit our lives. We get to reassess what we own. Is the rickety, rusty patio table worth repainting and storing one more time, or should I finally succumb and chuck it?

Weeding Out Possessions

My daughter just moved from Washington to Nantucket. Moving is not fun. You have to decide what to do with every single paper clip in your life. But the positive side is that a move forces you to examine what is and isn't important to carry with you through life. We don't have to move to do this, however.

Sometimes the cruelty of weather forces us to do it. Last winter our flooded basement and then the summer heat prompted "green crud growth" that rendered mundane objects indistinguishable. Out they went without a backward glance. Do you have boxes packed away in your attic that you haven't opened in years and don't know what's in them? Open them, assess the contents, and have a yard sale.

Some Good Advice

Getting organized is a personal thing. Where do we start and how does the pack rat or harried Harry and Harriet get it together? I discovered the best advice about getting organized from none other than Toni Morrison.

I read an article about this Pulitzer Prize–winning author in the magazine section of the Sunday New York *Times*. One paragraph lingered in my mind. When Ms. Morrison was a single mother, working full-time as an editor and trying to eke out a little time for writing, she was extremely bogged down in trivia. She was always confused about what to do next: Write a review, pick up groceries, help kids with homework, what? She took out a yellow pad and made a list of all the things she had to do. It included large things—being a good mother—and small things—calling the phone company. Then she made a list of the things she wanted to do. There were only two things without which she couldn't live; mothering her children and writing books. Then she cut out everything that didn't have to do with those two things and decided she didn't have the luxury to whine about not having time for anything that didn't relate to either of the two.

Start with a List

Because of limited space and a desire to keep everything, I've decided the best way to weed out is to make a list of the things I really need. I will then take stock, asking myself about each and every superfluous thing, "Do I really need this?" Unfortunately I have to work on my conscience because my answer is always the same. "No, but I really want it."

DECORATING TIPS FOR GETTING ORGANIZED

"Anyone can create a home office from a tiny space, freshen up a tired kitchen, find extra storage space, and update without remodeling. And, I'm going to show you how it can be done without spending a ton of money or a lot of time." This is my usual opening, or a variation of it, for my television appearances, and the more I do it the more enthusiastic I get about coming up with new ideas.

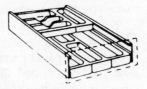

Winter is a good time to clean out forgotten drawers, one at a time. Make space by getting rid of the things you no longer use and concentrate on small changes that can make a big difference. The following ten tips should help.

Kitchen Clutter

Take everything out of your kitchen cabinets and drawers, one at a time. Remove everything you don't use, reline the drawers with fresh Contact paper and rearrange everything in the most convenient places. Your kitchen will seem a great deal larger and more efficient.

Storing It All

Customize your storage area with containers for holding everything neatly and in an attractive way. Add pretty labels to opaque jars. Put pastas, rice, and cereal in clear glass mason jars on the counter. They will look nice and you've cleared out some storage space. Do the same in your at-home office or sewing area.

Home Work

It may be a cliché, but it's still the easiest way to create an efficient desk for home office use. All it takes are two filing cabinets of the same height (but not necessarily the same style), a hollow-core door (about $22 at lumber yards) and three cans of spray paint, wood tone or faux finish, or clear polyurethane. Place the door on top of the file cabinets. Apply a finish to the desktop and refurbish ordinary desktop accessories with faux finishes. Add a lamp and a good swivel chair.

Scentsational!

Line closet shelves with scented paper and add a trim of satin ribbon glued to the front of each shelf. This simple little touch will make you feel enormously organized.

Quick Ties

Give plain panel curtains a fresh look with tiebacks made from a fat cord of braided silk in a rich color. It's sold by the yard in fabric or upholstery shops.

Faux Treasure

Team up a plain wooden disc, found in a home center, with a large terra cotta planter and you have the beginning of an interesting coffee table. Give the top a faux finish or painted stencil design and place it on top of the planter. If you want the look of textured stone, spray it with a granite finish. Nobody will guess it isn't the real thing!

From Plain to Pretty

Fancy, lace-edged bed linens are a lot more expensive than plain white, but if you buy them unadorned, it's a cinch to add your own eyelet, ribbon, or lace trim to the top edge, for a fraction of the cost.

Basketry

Use large baskets to hold magazines and books in the living room, personal items or rolled up towels in the bathroom, underwear in kids' rooms,

mittens and hats in the hall closet, toys in the rec room, gardening tools on the patio, sewing items, dried foods such as onions and garlic in the kitchen.

Freshen Up the Kitchen

Fill a wooden country utensil or window box with small potted herb plants or paper white bulbs and place on your kitchen windowsill. It will remind you of spring.

Seeing Red

Red is a cheerful color. But using it successfully for decorating can be tricky. Create a bright entryway with a shade of rich red paint. Since most hallways are devoid of windows, the red color will make it inviting and warm. You'll be surprised how many other colors go with it. This small change will instantly revitalize your decorating scheme.

ORGANIZING FOR ENTERTAINING

Having guests in the summertime can be fun or a nightmare. If you plan ahead and are organized, you'll all enjoy the experience. Guests can be the most considerate people in the world, but it still requires more trips to the supermarket, more meals to make, more beds to make ready, more beach towels to wash. There's only one way to ensure sanity—a well-organized household.

Baskets Are a Basic Must

I collect baskets of all sizes for the inevitable. The $3.95 laundry baskets are basic, good-looking and hold toys, towels, outdoor cushions, books, magazines, and other essentials that tend to pile up. If you need space for guests to put away clothing, these can work in the closet.

Prepare for Kids

I spend a lot of time in our local thrift shop storing up toys for all ages. Check out your Salvation Army and secondhand stores. You can often fill a bag of toys for a dollar. Fill a basket with coloring books, crayons, sticker books, and puzzles that are age appropriate for your guests' children.

Take Stock of Your Home

Before the onset of guests, take the time to fuss with things that need painting, sewing, recovering, or making. Take stock. Think about what your life is like when it's at its most hectic and how you can address the problem now. Fix, repair, spruce up what you know will bother you all summer if it isn't done, and make the time to do it beforehand.

Take Advantage of Pre-Summer

March is the month that everyone dreads because it's the last month before nice weather sets in. Make the most of it. Do indoor chores that you won't want to face once the weather gets really nice.

Finishing
Touches

LITTLE THINGS REALLY COUNT FOR A LOT

Every now and then I get the urge to spruce up. It isn't an overwhelming need to redecorate or to get involved in a long-term project, but just to put little touches on things. Lifting up the spirit of a room can do the same for the soul. Here are some ways to do this without committing your entire weekend to the process.

Paint

Paint small, occasional knickknack shelves a bright color. Then add a front trim with lace, rick-rack, or ribbon applied with double-faced tape. Arrange the shelves with brightly colored mugs, plates, and pitchers of fresh flowers.

From Plain to Pretty

Everyone has a plain pitcher, or you might find one at a yard sale. Jazz it up with colorful painted polka dots you apply at random with a cotton ball and permanent paint.

Add Storage Space

Mount wooden cubes on the bathroom wall to create extra shelf space for towels and personal items.

Pretty-Up the Bedroom
Make a bed coverlet in a patchwork pattern by stitching large cotton napkins together.

Details That Make a Difference
Make an ordinary dresser look up-to-date with interesting, new drawer pulls.

Shower in Style
Make a brightly patterned shower curtain. It's one of the easiest sewing projects that will instantly change the look of a room. No sewing skills? Use a single sheet with a border design. Add grommets evenly spaced across the top edge. The tool for setting them and the grommets come in a package at fabric and sewing stores, home centers, and paint and hardware stores.

Border It
Add a flower wallpaper border around a doorframe, window, or eating area in the kitchen. Use prepasted paper for greatest ease.

Herbs at Your Fingertips
Start an herb garden in a pretty pot on your kitchen counter. Or force bulbs to grow indoors. Every day brings a new surprise.

Trim Sensation
Paint the wood trim in one room with an unusual color you've always been attracted to. Try one of the new berry colors, deep green, or bright coral.

A Change of Pace
Rearrange the things you display on tables. Simplify, add picture frames, candle holders. Bring out the things you have tucked away and arrange them. Put away the things you've been looking at the most so you can forget them for awhile.

ALL THE TRIMMINGS

Trimmings are what turn an ordinary pillow, ottoman slipcover, or headboard into something extraordinary. You can achieve a designer look with an interesting trim for very little expense. In fact, you can add your own trim to a plain purchased pillow. You can even combine trims such as tassels with braided cord.

How to Do It

1. When stitching trim to fabric, use a zipper foot attachment on your sewing machine.
2. To help prevent raveling while you work, wrap tape around the cut ends of braided cording.
3. If sewing around a pillow or other item with corners, make a snip into the seam allowance of the trim fabric just before you get to the corner. In this way the fabric can be turned easily.
4. Ends of the trim should meet without overlapping. If you're working with piping, the ends of the cord should meet with the fabric then covering and overlapping itself.
5. Begin and end the trim in the middle of the bottom side of a pillow, not at a corner.

Creative Uses

1. Use trims to tie accessories together. For example, use the same trim around a wastebasket, lamp shade, throw pillows, table-cloth, and bedskirt.
2. Tie back curtains with fringed tassel cords.
3. Attach tassels to the corners of pillows.
4. Glue thin braid around picture frames, vases, lamp bases.

5. Edge a piece of tapestry with thick gold braid and hang on the wall.
6. Use trimmings to tie up napkins.
7. Glue trim around the edge of a room-divider screen.
8. Use several rows of covered cording to create an interesting edging all around a room where the wall and ceiling meet.
9. Trims have always been used at Christmastime. Use them to decorate Styrofoam balls.
10. Embellish plain curtains with a tassel fringe in a color to match your fabric for a custom-made look.

 # CREATING A MOOD

There is more to enjoying one's environment than the way it looks. Comfort is part of good interior design, but there are other things involved with creating a pleasing place in which to live. To some, a room is totally bare if there are no fresh flowers. Many people have plants and trees as part of their decor. And to others, no home is complete without sound. Music, that is. No matter how you introduce music to your home, for added pleasure give some thought to matching your musical selection to the activity.

Set the Scene for a Formal Dinner

Selecting the right music for the mood you want to create is an art. The addition of music at a party adds to the festive feeling just as much as the food, the table setting, the furnishings, and the flowers. Imagine a formal candlelit dinner. The table is set with a black-and-white theme—white candles in clear glass candle-holders or hurricane lamps, white placemats or linen tablecloth, and black napkins. There are four perfect freesias in the center of a white or clear glass bowl. What's needed is a selection of classical music to round out the ambience.

Informality

For a barbecue on the deck, use a different color place setting for each person with colorful bandanas for napkins. Lively music sets the mood here.

Country Style

For a country brunch, set the table with a blue-and-white theme. You might use checked or plaid placemats with blue-and-white-checkered napkins tied in a knot. Add fresh white daisies in a white crock or pitcher for the centerpiece, and fill a white bowl with fresh strawberries and another with blueberries. The background music might be the musical score from a favorite show like *Oklahoma.*

Working to Music

Some people do their best work when classical music is playing in the office. Others prefer popular tunes for stimulation. Still others work best to a favorite Broadway musical score. Music is a very personal thing and most anyone will answer immediately when asked to name his or her favorite recording artist.

Hidden Music

A music system can be as simple or elaborate as suits your needs. There are in-the-wall systems for incorporating music into your interior design and speakers so small they aren't obtrusive.

A BIT OF OPULENCE

Comfort, opulence, and extravagance are qualities we often yearn for when we take stock of our own rooms. I always come home from a showhouse tour with the desire to get rid of everything I own and start over. But you don't have to redo every room or spend lots of money to create the feeling of luxury in a room. Here are some quick tricks to create the illusion you're after with the use of accessories.

Pillows

My favorite item for changing the look of a room is the throw pillow. For pure luxury, add large (22- to 24-inch square) sink-into pillows made from vintage fabrics—velvet, silk, brocade and tapestry, or pretty floral chintz. The addition of trim like braid or silk tassels or fat piping will further enhance the pillows. Use two large pillows at either end of your sofa, rather than three or four small ones. If you can't afford to buy the really nice ones, consider making your own. A pillow is probably one of the easiest sewing projects and you'll need less than a yard of fabric. Buy the soft pillow forms that feel like down.

Curtain Tiebacks

If you're making pillows, buy extra fabric to make curtain tiebacks to match. This is another easy sewing project that will enhance your room. If you have simple plain curtain panels, the addition of a tieback with a pretty finial to hold it in place (not a cup hook) will give your window treatment a finished look. I like them to be about 4 to 6 inches wide, depending on the width of your curtain, and about half as long as the width of the curtain. When making them always line the strip with interfacing to give it body.

Cut Flowers

Fresh flowers in beautiful clear glass vases help to create an air of luxury in any room. This is a small expense for a big impact. When possible use large vases with just a few long-stemmed flowers. For example, fill a large white bowl with six sprigs of freesia. They are light and delicate and give off a wonderful scent. Use either all white flowers such as tulips, or a combination of flowers that reflect a dominant color in the room.

Fresh Coat of Paint

For the quickest, easiest makeover, give a room a fresh coat of paint. Dark rooms seem more luxurious than light rooms. They are more dramatic and richer looking. Sometimes they even seem cozier and there is a softer, more peaceful quality about them.

Deep green is a good color to create this effect. Dark brown or deep gray are other choices. Paint the molding and window trim eggshell or stark white. Red is another color to consider for an opulent look, but you may find it a difficult color to live with.  You have to love it. When painting with a dark color, use semigloss or even add a glaze to the latex paint. It will give it a richer finish and protect the walls from scuff marks.

Gold

Gilded mirrors, picture frames, candlesticks, even chair frames all introduce the look of opulence. For a table setting, use white chinaware with a gold rim.

Floor Covering

Oriental and Persian area carpets make a room look luxurious. While the real thing is quite expensive, a good reproduction will give the room the same feeling and hardly anyone will know the difference. Surprisingly, these rugs, filled with pattern and color, look good with any furniture or fabric and are especially nice on a wood floor. If you live in a warm climate you might consider a good Kilim or Indian rug.

Table Settings

When you entertain, take out all your wedding gifts of silver and chinaware. Don't leave them tarnishing and gathering dust in a cupboard. Also use nice linens. I like to set a table with a long linen tablecloth over which I place a tea cloth of pure white linen edged with lace, or an eggshell crocheted tablecloth I inherited from my grandmother. Use little crystal salt dishes and silver candlesticks (only white candles please!). A table can't be overset.

Bedroom

I say this over and over, but it's worth repeating here, no bed can have too many pillows. Combine square pillows, neckrolls, and oversized leaning pillows. Cover them with wonderful lacy or soft pastel brocade shams. Cover the bed with a puffy down comforter in winter or a soft white mohair blanket in warmer weather. Pure white cotton sheets are a must even if you have others as well. For soft comfort and luxurious looks, white is the answer.

Finishing Touches

Wallpaper, borders, and trims are the finishing touches that make a room look finished. Shop for tassel fringes, braided rope, colored gimp, and ribbon in fabric and upholstery shops. These decorative items can be added to any plain fabric—around a pillow, edging a tablecloth, along the border of a curtain, edging sheets, towels, and slipcovers. Plain becomes instantly elegant.

 # MOLDING

Adding molding is one of the easiest home improvement projects you can do to add instant character to a room. Most people think that molding only hides the raw edges where the walls and ceiling or floors meet, but molding is also used for decoration. All sorts of molding trims, both decorative and straight, narrow and wide, are sold in lumber stores and home centers.

Adding Character

Apply elegant detailed molding around the top of a room with high ceilings to create architectural interest where none exists. Molding can also be applied at baseboards or around doors and windows. Add a decorative wainscoting or chair rail in a dining room and wallpaper above or below. It should be installed between 33 and 35 inches from the floor. The molding can be stained or painted.

Tools to Do It Yourself

You'll need a hack saw in a miter box to cut proper angles, a hammer, finishing nails in various sizes, a nail set for counter sinking the finishing nail below the surface, a twenty-five foot metal ruler or tape measure, and wood filler, glue, and sandpaper. The most common finishing nails to use with molding are 3d (1^1/$_2$ inch) and 4d (1^1/$_2$ inch).

How to Do It

Measure the length of each wall twice. Round up each measurement to the next full foot and then add a foot to ensure extra length for mitering. If a wall measures ten feet five inches, round up to eleven feet and add another foot for a total of twelve feet. Mismeasurement is the most common problem for amateurs and professionals and can be costly. Better to waste a few inches than have to throw away the entire piece because you're short.

Molding comes in lengths from six to sixteen feet. Most interior trim is made up of 8-foot sections. To splice wood molding, miter two 45-degree angles, joining them with glue and nails. This is known as a "scarf joint."

Different Molding Types

Basic molding for ceilings is called stop, cove, bed, and crown. For chair rails it's often called batten or colonial casing, and for the baseboard it's called picture, half-round, and base-shoe molding. Don't be limited by one kind. It's possible to combine different styles to create your own design.

Simply Good Looking

The simplest design for baseboard molding is a flat base, usually four to six inches high and one inch thick, which is placed against the wall on the floor. A one-quarter round base mold is then butted against the flat base at the floor, creating a decorative baseboard.

Framed Fireplace

You can use any style of molding around a fireplace. Create an elaborate mantle where none exists by combining different molding styles until you come up with a design that looks good and is the right proportion for your fireplace.

Outdoors

You may not realize that you can use decorative molding outdoors as well. Use it to highlight screen doors, entranceways, and garage doors, or to create a door plaque for your address. Use Thompson's Exterior Water Seal Stain or outdoor paint on wood that is exposed to weather.

Details

Georgia-Pacific has an extensive line of molding polyurethane trims called Details Architectural Millwork that is great for a house facade because it won't succumb to weather conditions. You get the look of wood without the maintenance. Details millwork won't rot, warp, splinter, or split. It also won't attract termites or carpenter ants. There's entrance trim, window trim, decorative millwork like rosettes and brackets, and detailed moldings for windows, doors, and porches. I like the gingerbread trim you see in the south. Even though it's finished you can still paint it with one coat of your own color latex or oil base paint and it's easy to install with the directions that come with it.

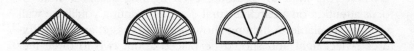

Patterns

Georgia-Pacific has the details for decorative entranceways like acorn pediments, fluted pilasters, and elliptical and half-round sunbursts for over the doorway or windows. These are just a few of the ornamentations available. You can create the look of colonial homes, Southern mansions, or Victorian charm. If you want to know more, call 1-800/BUILD-GP for a free consumer brochure called "Details Make the Difference."

 LIGHTING

 Lighting is always the last consideration when remodeling or decorating a room. But it can be the most important finishing element in a successful completion. In fact, lighting can change the mood of a room and create an ambience that is appropriate for the activities done in that room. When the lighting is all wrong, too harsh or not bright enough, it is immediately apparent and bothersome. Here are some tips from the American Lighting Association.

Even Lighting

When you want to distribute even lighting across a wall, or focus attention on an architectural detail or painting you'll use wall washers, available in lighting showrooms. Recessed and track fixtures reflect light and should be placed about two to three feet from the wall with as much space between them.

Spotlighting

When you want to emphasize an area, you'll install recessed downlights or track heads about a foot from the wall with the same space between. Spotlights should aim straight down so the light grazes the wall.

Lighting on a Low Budget

If you're on a tight budget you can achieve dramatic lighting effects with an uplight. It's a floor can that comes in black or white (some stores carry it in colors), costs about $15, and is approximately seven to eight inches high. It's perfect for lighting dark corners, for lighting a plant, or for brightening a dark corner. Use a 60-watt incandescent bulb.

Artificial Sunlight

Halogen lighting is truer to sunlight than incandescent or fluorescents. Halogen lights are being used more and more for illuminating counter space and desk work.

Outdoor
Living

LUSH AND INVITING PORCHES

No Southern home would be complete without a summer porch. However, this outdoor living room seems to have become an added attraction in all climates, even if it's used for only two or three months of the year. Porches are romantic. A summer porch evokes an image of lazy days, sprawling out on chaises, sipping lemonade. Even porches found on grand and formal homes have an air of relaxed comfort. This is the only way to furnish a porch.

Relaxed and Comfy

The furniture on a porch doesn't have to match, it doesn't have to be new, it doesn't have to be anything but comfortable. When you or your guests plunk down on a sofa or sink into a chair there should be no concern over whether or not you will mess it up. The mood should always be informal. This is what a porch represents. You might have museum-quality pieces in the rest of the house, but the porch is for slouching.

Getting That Informal Look

All it takes to get that great "lived in" look is informal arranging. For me, outdoor living is synonomous with a wide wraparound porch on a typical New England farmhouse. In Key West, Florida, porches are delineated by gingerbread trim and often reflect a decidedly Bahamian influence. There is always a hammock attached to one corner post and to the house wall. Pillows thrown casually about give a porch a lived-in look. I prefer blue-and-white ticking or plaid fabric that looks tucked rather than fitted on cushions. I also like pillows that are oversized and plain. Save the ruffles, piping, or other trims for the living room. Soft Touch™ pillow forms give pillows that sinkable look and feeling.

Porch Colors

White seems to be the most popular color for painting a porch. Decking is usually dove gray or Cape Cod gray, but Newport blue is another preferred color. In the South I often see porch ceilings painted light blue or aqua, but lavender can be quite pretty as well.

Fabric

Fabric that has been treated for weather resistance is always practical, but I like the feel of chintz or sheeting. Scotchgard-treated fabric will resist stains, and spilled drinks will bead up rather than soak into it. You'll usually find this information somewhere on the fabric when you buy it. Sheets feel cool in summer and they are practical for making your own cushion and pillow covers. The Ralph Lauren and Liz Claiborne lines are particularly pretty, and you can often find them discounted in places like Bed, Bath, and Beyond.

Porches with a View

When you sit outside on a porch it's nice to have a view even if you create it yourself. For example, you can grow climbing roses on posts or on a fence surrounding the porch. In this way, take advantage of the natural colors and echo the design on your fabrics. You can also stencil a design on your floor, furniture, or planters to bring color into your decorating scheme. Decorator Blocks™ from Plaid Enterprises allow you to create the look of handpainting (similar to stamping a design onto a surface, only better) for interesting accessories. Or, you can create a painted vine that winds around porch railings where no plantings exist.

Whitewashing Trees

I had never before seen this done, but you can whitewash the trunks of trees. This is done to prevent insects from going up the trunks but serves as a decorative touch as well. Then plant lovely white flowers around the tree trunk for a simple, elegant porch surround.

Trellises

If you have a blank wall on the porch, consider adding a trellis. You can purchase a premade trellis from any garden center and attach it easily to any wall. Create pots of climbing flowers within the porch area for an indoor garden oasis.

A friend of mine built a porch with an open trellis for the roof over which he grew a grape vine tree. It has spread over the trellis to form a protected natural "ceiling" that allows dappled light to seep in, but provides shade and protection. It is quite lovely when in bloom.

Floor Covering

Floorcloths made of artist's canvas and then painted or faux-finished are currently quite popular. Years ago they came into being because people couldn't afford rugs and wanted something of interest on the floor. Today, artisans create beautifully painted, illustrated, and finished floorcloths that can easily cost more than carpeting a room. However, there are many that are affordable and you can make one yourself for very little. This is a nice touch on a porch. Or you can stencil a border around the porch for added interest.

Flowers

Lots and lots of plants will give your porch the feeling of a delightful garden room. Choose plant containers of different sizes and heights and fill with flowers that match your color scheme. Or, do the reverse. Choose the fabrics and paint to match the flowers that are in  season. Whimsical floral prints and paintings can be lovely on a porch wall. Keep it lively. Nothing serious on the porch. Arrange pressed flowers under a glasstop table for something different.

Yard Sale Finds

If you find old wicker or wooden furniture that needs to be refurbished consider sponge painting. It hides a multitude of sins and is easier to apply than a good coat of paint. You begin by painting the surface, but it doesn't have to be a super job. Next mix equal parts of the same paint (oil base, water base, indoor or outdoor), with Formby's Decorative Touches Sponge Glaze Mix. Using a natural sponge, dab the mixture all over the object. Continue to do this until you like the effect. It's amazingly simple to do and the results are always terrific!

THE HOTTEST COLORS FOR COOL OUTDOOR DECORATING

A deck extends our living space tremendously. And decorating the deck is an ideal way to bring the indoors out with the same sense of color displayed in the interior design of your home. If you want an outdoor living room that will look smart and chic for the next two years you can't go wrong with back-to-nature colors.

Starting from the Bottom Up

Start with the deck. Just as you might choose a carpet color to dictate the direction for decorating your living room, now you can do the same with your deck. Did you know you can waterproof and add color to your deck at the same time with Thompson's Exterior Color Stains? In fact, you can even add a design, such as a border around the deck, with a stencil pattern and coordinating stain colors. For an attractive contemporary look, use two contrasting light and dark stain colors to create an overall checkerboard pattern or even a pattern that looks like an "area rug." It's easy to apply and you'll have a decorative and striking background on which to arrange your outdoor furniture.

Bordering on Color

If you're a traditionalist and simply want a good-looking, weatherproof deck, coat it with Thompson's Cape Cod Gray color stain. Then add excitement by using an accent color on the benches, planters, or fence around the deck. This might be forest green, or mossy green. Staining wooden planters is a good way to add an up-to-date look in strategic spots around the deck. It's also a nice way to enhance flowering plants.

Checkerboard How-To's

To create a checkerboard pattern on your deck, use a light and dark stain. After choosing your colors, apply the lighter color to the entire deck as per directions on the can. Next, measure and draw a checkerboard pattern of approximately 8 to 10 inch squares over the entire deck. Then apply the darker stain color to every other square. You might find that using a strip of masking tape around each square will ensure perfect delineation. Practice on a plain board before starting the deck project.

A Modern Look

Once you've created a colorful deck it's time to consider the furnishings. If you're tired of the inexpensive plastic chairs from discount centers, now is the time to invest in some good-looking outdoor furniture. The Brown Jorden line of chaise longues, tables, and dining chairs are sleek, carefree, weather-resistant, and comfortable. They are also sturdy and will last for a very long time. To dress up the environment mix in a few throw pillows in a variety of earth tones to match the deck colors.

Recreating the Past

Lloyd Flanders outdoor wicker chairs are reminiscent of the 1920s and they come with their own weather-resistant, fabric-covered cushions. A grouping of these chairs, which come in various sizes and shapes, will create an instant environment for lazy summer afternoons. Add a few throw pillows in an overall calico print for color and comfort. If you live in an area where the night air is moist, keep a large basket with a handle on the deck for gathering the pillows up to take in at night. Then it's easy to take them out in the morning and spread them about.

Dining with a Bit of Dash

A pretty and practical dining area is easy to create with an unfinished wooden table and stain. This would be the perfect project to stencil with a border around the outer edge, or create an overall pattern that looks like a tablecloth. You might even have fun making patterns that look like placemats as part of the tablecloth. You can create a table that's not only interesting and unique but also totally waterproof.

Colorful How-To's

Select a stain color for the background. It might be a light color such as cream, driftwood, or gray. Follow the directions on the can and apply to all exposed surfaces of the table. Home centers and art supply stores carry a wide variety of precut stencil designs for all sorts of uses. You can find designs that are suitable for a border as well as an overall pattern. You might like to use a geometric design or one that is less formal, such as rambling vines or small floral buds.

Next, choose the color stains for the stencil designs. If your pattern includes vines or leaves, evergreen would be appropriate. If you have a pattern of roses, use red or pink. Lemon is especially pretty when used over Cape Cod gray, pewter, or Newport blue. Use a sponge brush to apply the color stain onto the stencil cutouts. Do this by dipping the brush into the stain, then wipe the excess stain off onto newspaper before dabbing it onto the stencil. Let each area dry before moving the stencil pattern and continuing to add stain all around the table. You can apply this same technique to the deck but you will probably choose a larger-scale design than that which you might use on the table. Once finished, the furniture or deck will be completely waterproof. Be sure to coat all exposed wood, such as the underside of the table and the legs as well.

When you've finished your colorful stain projects, filled the planters, and arranged a few pretty pillows, you can sit back, relax, and enjoy a beautiful, carefree summer.

SUMMER DRESSING

It's easy to spruce up your deck for summer living. The word to remember when choosing fabrics, furniture, and table settings is "carefree." Summertime means that you don't have to spend a lot of time maintaining.

This year, I ordered yards and yards of fabrics for making pillows and cushions and tablecovers for color and comfort on the deck. Pale colors work best in the Northeast where I live, but when we go to Key West, Florida, I can't help but be influenced by the brilliant sunlight. Surrounded by tropical palms and flowering plants in fuchsia, bright orange, lemony citrus, and a host of other riotous colors, the pale hues look washed out. But it's fun to try both approaches, so here are simple ways to try out different colors.

Sheet Savvy

Places like Kmart sell inexpensive polyester sheets in a variety of bright colors. They might be too stiff or too garish for comfort on a bed, but they are great for making economical and practical pillow covers for porch lounging. Don't even think about ruffles and fat cording or braid trims that look tailored or stiff. Cut out large, 22- to 24-inch squares, stitch them up, and stuff them. I like "Soft Touch" pillow forms from Fairfield Processing Corp. because they feel like down but are reasonably priced. The finished pillows will have a squooshy, sink-into look. Throw them around the deck for easy lounging and they'll add bright spots here and there. The polyester material resists dampness even if it isn't completely waterproof.

Poolside

Colorful, inexpensive towels provide another material for pillow covers. These are especially good by a pool. Simply fold the towel so one end flaps over the other. Stitch up two sides (the ends are finished), insert a polyfoam pillow form, and add corresponding Velcro tabs to the flap for closing. Combine colors to match plants in colorful pots and you'll have an instant "look."

Green, Green, and Greener

Green in all shades is always in style for an outdoor living room. Forest, teal, turquoise, hunter, fern, and pale baby aqua can all be mixed together with accents of bright white.

Try a combination of green and white with accents of butterscotch yellow. Plaids, checks, and stripes are teamed for a winning look. Deck stains come in all different colors and are being used on outdoor furniture. A chair stained in lemonwood is teamed with another stained in apple green. Add pillows in green-and-white and yellow-and-white checks of different sizes.

Formal Isn't Cool

Formal outdoor furniture is definitely gone. I love the look of wicker; a rocking chair here, a plant holder there, even a chaise longue. If you have wicker or wrought iron, mix them with some funky, odd pieces of furniture found at yard  sales. Give them a coat of waterproof stain or outdoor paint and faux-finish or stencil on a design. Adirondack chairs are classic and you can do all sorts of things to make them more interesting as well as comfortable. They are indestructible and seem to get better with age. Container gardening makes it easy to move things around every time you want a new look. Try to find unusual things at the home center to use or refinish for planters.

SEW FOR OUTDOORS

Wow! You can easily laminate any fabric with a new-to-the-market kit. Imagine being able to use the same fabric you have on your sofa indoors on your cushions outdoors. Now you can sew slipcovers, chair cushions, pillows, tablecloths, and placemats for outdoors.

Laminated Fabrics

Fabric companies are now offering a wide array of prints in water- and mildew-resistant laminated fabrics. According to the Sewing Fashion Council, which represents the American Home Sewing and Craft Association, today's glossy or matte-laminated fabrics retain their texture and flexibility, and are a breeze to clean with a damp cloth. If your heart is set on a particular fabric that isn't available as a laminate, the new iron-on laminates give any fabric, even linen, the water-resistant characteristics you want while retaining the tactile qualities of fabric. Local fabric stores should carry the iron-on laminates.

Color, Color Everywhere

Your fabric print and color choices are limitless, and you can even add trims to the laminated pillow fabric or around the bottom of the table cover. So spruce up the patio or deck with a riot of color, or beautiful florals or blue-and-white checks (my favorite) and don't worry about the fabric getting ruined.

Cover the Unsightlies

There's nothing beautiful about looking at a grill sitting in the middle of your beautiful backyard. It's easy to make a cover for it with a laminated fabric to match the rest of your furniture. If you have expensive patio or pool furniture, make covers for them with a pattern from McCall's or Vogue.

Do It Yourself

McCall's and Vogue have teamed up with Waverly and show some pretty ideas in their pattern books.

There are patterns available for making a round tablecloth, for making pillows in all sizes and shapes (for a porch swing, for example), for a chaise longue cushion, and for slipcovers for indoor as well as outdoor furniture. You might consider using the laminated fabric indoors for carefree maintenance as well. And it can't be beat for a sunroom. You can buy these patterns where fabrics are sold.

Tools of the Trade

While at the fabric store, check the notions section for tools that will make your sewing project even easier. Products that make working with laminates easier are a walking (even-feed), Teflon-coated or roller foot for your sewing machine to prevent sticking or slipping. Weights or clips are helpful to secure fabrics for cutting. Use nylon or polyester thread, which is stronger and more resistant to weather, mold, and mildew—particularly for outdoor use. To create invisible stitches, use a medium-weight monofilament thread.

Choose heavy-duty needles, size 70 or 80, that are made for home decorating projects and change them when they become dull. Because pinholes break the waterproofing boundary, use pins only in seam allowances and make a 1/2-inch or wider seam allowance.

Bargain
Shopping

Bargain Bests

I can't pass by a secondhand store, flea market, yard sale, or Salvation Army or thrift shop without checking it out. I have the same affinity for discount and five-and-ten-cent stores like Kmart and Woolworth's. But my favorite haunts are hardware and home centers. When a salesperson asks if he or she can help me find an item, the answer is always the same, "I'm not sure what I'm looking for." I walk up and down the aisles looking for objects that could be used in ways for which they were not intended. For example, the boating section yields all sorts of interesting hardware that would be ideal for drawer pulls, curtain tie-backs, and whatever else I can think up in an instant. Sometimes, if a good-looking item seems inexpensive, I'll take it home knowing an idea for a creative use will come to me in time.

Stepping Up

Small wooden step ladders cost about $9. They are made of sturdy raw wood. They are utilitarian, not meant for decoration. However, when given a coat of bright paint, or even faux-finished, this item is adorable as a plant holder. Just add little potted plants on each step and place it inside or out on a deck or patio.

Framed

Frames in different sizes and shapes are always provocative when grouped together on a wall. Some can be fitted with mirrors, others can be used to frame photographs or prints. They are easy to find, especially if they aren't in good condition. Some frames look good even with the paint peeling off, others look better with a new coat of paint, some gold leafing, a sponge-painted finish, or sanded and left raw. All these treatments are easy enough for anyone to do and the cost is minimal.

Kitchen Cabinets

For an inexpensive kitchen update, cut a louvered door in half, add knobs, and use as cabinet doors. Paint them white or sponge-paint them in light and dark shades of eggshell. Round porcelain knobs or U-shaped handles will give the doors a modern look.

Fabric Ends

Remnants of fabric are always on sale. These end pieces are often large enough to make all sorts of home accessories like pillows, patchwork wallhangings, napkins, and placemats. Use a variety and mix and match for interest.

Mirrors

One of the decade's popular finds in antique stores is an old window with many panes that have been replaced with mirrors. The shabbier the frame the more interesting. Window frames come in all sizes and shapes. If you find one that appeals to you, take it to any home center that cuts glass and they will outfit the frames with mirrors. This is a terrific item for a hallway.

CREATIVE BUYING

You don't have to spend a lot of money to put together a stylish environment. In fact, cheap chic is really in. It's just knowing how to keep an eye out for great bargains.

"Take It or Leave It"

In our own town we have a "Take It Or Leave It" section at the dump, or, rather "landfill," which is now the politically correct reference. Sunday morning is the best time to go because all the unsold items from Saturday's yard sales end up here. It's a regular coffee klatch meeting place without the coffee. While searching through junk, you can exchange gossip with your neighbors. Here you find perfectly good items, some brand new along with the indescribables, waiting for the right creative eye to spot them. I love this sort of challenge. So do hundreds of others, millionaires among them. Money has nothing to do with the thrill of finding a treasure in someone else's trash.

Creative Chairs

Wooden chairs are easy to find, but they're rarely in perfect condition. Sometimes a rung is missing, but most often the seat is gone. Replacing a rung or a seat isn't a difficult repair job and

 chairs are ripe for creative finishing. While driving down a street in Key West, I spotted four chairs in a storefront window. These were reclaimed wooden bridge-type chairs and each was painted a bright color. All the seats had been recovered with cherry red vinyl and the chairs were painted bright blue, purple, lime green, and fuchsia. Only one cross piece of each chair back was painted a different color to match one of the other chairs. For example, the bright fuchsia had one spoke painted in the lime green, while the purple had a fuchsia spoke.

The painting was beautifully done and I thought this an interesting approach to making ordinary chairs extraordinary.

Unpainted Chairs

Chairs with years of paint peeling away are often discarded. For those who understand, a peeling chair finish can be absolutely charming. Don't use it for seating, but rather for holding an enamel coffeepot filled with a bouquet of field flowers. It is the quintessential symbol of a lazy summer afternoon.

Enamelware

Whether in good condition or chipped, enamel pots, mugs, colandars, and pitchers are back in style. Use them to hold flowers, wooden spoons, and other kitchen utensils for a delightful touch of country. The more you have, the better. They make a wonderful display on open kitchen shelves and could lead to a collection.

Collectibles

DECORATING WITH ARTWORK

Tips for Buying Art

Buying art can be tricky. Many people are intimidated in a way they never are when buying other home furnishings. They don't trust their judgment when it comes to art. Here are some tips that will help.

Choosing Art

The most obvious questions people ask themselves are:

1. Will it look good in my dining room?
2. Will it fit over the sofa?
3. Should I buy a print or a painting?
4. What size should it be?

Men Versus Women

It's a curious thing to compare the buying habits of men and women. You wouldn't think of this as a gender thing, but more often than not men buy what they like, while women are more calculating about practical considerations like size, color, and where it will go. They also think about how others will view the new art piece and what overall effect it will have on their decorating scheme.

Still other women will consult the artist about matters of interior design, especially when it comes to color.

What to Do and What Not to Do

1. Don't buy on impulse.
2. Go back often to see a painting in different lighting. Artificial light can change the color from what the painting looked like in daylight.
3. Don't bargain shop. If you like an artist's work the price is less important than the piece. You will always find something in your price range that you like.
4. Do not buy art as a gift unless it is something small. A miniature of a favorite painting or print will always fit somewhere, but giving someone a large important piece of artwork can be embarrassing for the recipient.
5. Many people buy small artwork for college students. This is a good way to introduce a young person to art without a major investment.

 # FRAMING

Almost anything can be framed: old high school diplomas, antique photographs, letters, caricatures, wedding certificates, birth announcements, cross stitching, children's drawings. And when framed properly these items can make wonderful and personal gifts. At most home centers like Builder's Square they have more than three hundred colorful mats to match almost any color.

Color Is Key

Color is the most important key to selecting the perfect mat and frame. If there's a little color in a picture, then it's best to match the mat and frame colors to either the color scheme in the room where it will hang or to the furniture color scheme.

Style of the Frame

You can match the frame to the style of your furniture. Some frames are quite simple, while others are very ornate. Take the time to choose the right frame for the artwork.

Framing Experts

While there are materials for do-it-yourself framing, it's an exacting science that takes time. If you want your item to look professionally framed, have it done by a professional.

FAMILY PHOTOGRAPHS

We all take lots of photographs. Some are worth putting in an album, some get thrown in a drawer, others we send to family members and some we actually frame for hanging or to display on furniture. Creative Memories is a national photo-preservation program with some simple solutions and techniques for people who want to organize and preserve their photos and memorabilia. They offer the following tips for selecting safe albums and adhesives, choose methods for organizing years of photos, and crop photos for the most effective picture.

1. Use acid-free albums and don't store negatives in a photo album or with photos.
2. Store photos in 65- to 70-degree temperature with a realitive humidity of 40 percent.
3. Take a roll of black-and-white photos every year (they last longer than color).
4. Keep framed pictures out of direct sunlight.
5. Add memorabilia and written documentation to your photo collections.

Family Celebrations

My mother is about to have an important milestone birthday and my daughter came up with the perfect gift from the whole family. We bought a pretty album with lots of insert pages. Then we sent a page to each person to fill with photos or memorabilia that related to times spent with my mother. We then assembled all the pages and made up a cover page with photos representing a table of contents. We will all gather for a birthday party at which time we'll present the album.

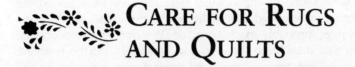 # CARE FOR RUGS AND QUILTS

Many people collect early country folk art. Quilts and hooked rugs are among the most popular, perhaps because these are two of America's truly indigenous crafts. More and more fine examples of these needle arts seem to surface as they are being appreciated for their age and simple charm. But caring for and repairing these sometimes fragile pieces of history can be a problem.

Quilts

When an old quilt becomes torn or worn out, it can be impossible to repair. Sometimes the fabric of an old quilt is too fragile to sew. Many collectors have been known to cut up old quilts, salvaging the good parts to make into pillow covers.

1. Replacing a worn patch of fabric might require washing and bleaching new fabric in order to match the faded shades of the original.
2. Backing a patch with a fusible webbing such as Stitch Witchery can create body under the new piece, making it easier to stitch it to the worn fabric backing.
3. A quilt that is hung on a wall where it is exposed to direct sunlight will surely fade. Sometimes, a new quilt that is allowed to fade will take on the quality of an old quilt and add to its charm.

4. An old quilt should be washed in the bathtub with mild detergent, then rinsed and rolled in a terry cloth towel. Then hang it out to dry on a sunny day. Do not expect an old quilt to hold up in the washing machine and dryer. Dry cleaning is not recommended. If the quilt isn't very old you might consider washing it with cold water on a gentle cycle in the machine. But first test the colorfastness of the fabric to be sure it won't bleed.

Hooked Rugs

Many rugmakers began their craft by repairing a family heirloom. Fortunately, they realized the value of the rugs they found and had the sense to restore them. So many rugs were lost to future generations of appreciators because they were tossed out by unknowing souls who thought they were just some old, torn, useless rugs, probably machine made. Perhaps it never occurred to them that rugs, even those in bad condition, can be restored. Often, if the restorer is experienced, even the most discerning collector can't tell where the old and new meet.

Here's some advice from the experts:

1. Some rugs are beyond repair. If you fall in love with a rug that isn't in perfect condition, hold it up to the light. If it's filled with holes it may have dry rot and will surely fall apart. This sort of disrepair is impossible to fix.
2. If you have a rug that needs restoring, it's important to find someone who knows exactly how to handle the job. It helps if the restorer is a fine sewer. One restorer attributes her expert craftsmanship in rug restoration to her background in haute couture.
3. When your rug needs cleaning, don't send it to just any dry cleaner. There are some that know how to handle them with care. This is very important. Get references if you want to be absolutely certain.
4. Don't vacuum the rug, but rather place it face down and use a brush to sweep it.
5. Sunning and airing rugs from time to time is a good idea.
6. Never shake a rug. If it is very old it may fall apart right in your hands. The burlap is so much weaker than the wool that it often disintegrates.
7. If washing is needed, do so a section at a time using a soft

brush and cold, slightly soapy water. Do not wring it out or hang it up to dry. With the front side out, roll the rug in a heavy towel to absorb the moisture, then roll it out flat to dry.

8. If you find a wonderful old rug that is too delicate to use, it can be bound and mounted for framing. It's important to mount a rug carefully and properly for even weight distribution.

9. When storing a rug or quilt, never fold it or put it in an airtight plastic bag. It is best to roll it with the front side out and wrap it with a sheet or cloth for protection.

10. A rug that is used on the floor will last longer and stay in better condition if you put it on top of another carpet or use a rubber pad beneath it.

11. Keep valuable and delicate rugs out of high-traffic areas. Dirt, mud, spills, and sunlight are enemies of your hooked rugs.

Changes for
the Seasons

FRESHEN UP, IT'S SPRING!

The Kip's Bay Decorator Showhouse in Manhattan is always the crème de la crème of showhouses and the best designers showcase their work here. It made me drool over many items I wanted but knew I could never afford. Many of us are tired of being told how to have a perfectly beautiful home. It takes effort. It's hard to live a normal life and keep a house looking like it came from the pages of a magazine. So it isn't surprising that so many people are embracing the idea of cheap chic, or eclectic style. Let's face it, it's just more comfortable to create a combination of things you find and love.

My house is relaxed at the moment. By this I mean there are things around that creep into the place and shouldn't be here. There are books, magazines, and newspapers on chairs and tables. My china cabinet is brimming with too many uninteresting things, obliterating the carefully arranged chinaware. I give myself permission to let things get out of hand from time to time. I just can't let it go on too long or it might become a permanent state of being.

In January I rearranged and got the place respectable enough for a magazine feature, something I do periodically. Once the photographs were taken everything went back to "normal." Nobody, I discovered, can live in a magazine set. But I like it when things are pretty. It gives me pleasure to walk through rooms that are well designed, where furniture is carefully placed. So what are we to do? I plan to come up with a good solution to this, but for the moment I will simply have to stop complaining or start rearranging.

Getting Inspiration

If you have a yearning to replace, redecorate, or rearrange, you might like to know that the trend is leaning toward a spare, rather monochromatic look. Get inspiration by going through the home furnishings stores in your area. Even if you can't afford to redecorate the whole house, add a few occasional pillows made from vintage fabrics to your sofa, drape a soft mohair throw over a chair, and exchange your old coffee table for a wrought iron garden table and you'll have an instant new look. Fill a basket with pots of primroses for a splash of color and your house will seem fresh with very little effort. This is what I did when I was creating spring in January. My house looked good enough for a magazine story, if only for a few days! I intend to do it again—very soon.

EVERYTHING'S COMING UP ROSES

What is it about roses that makes us so attracted to them? We plant them in the garden. We choose rose fabric for our furniture. We buy bedroom ensembles with a rose theme. And we never tire of them. Year after year we find roses the topic of not only gardening magazines, but also of interior design magazines and books. Roses are the wedding flower of choice. One of the reasons they never wear out their welcome is there are so many different varieties and colors. This is one flower that is endlessly fascinating and always guaranteed to please.

Freshly Picked

Nothing fills the house with such gentle fragrance as a freshly picked bouquet of roses. One sprig of rosa rugosa in a little cut glass vase is all you need to bring springtime into a powder room. Mix different colored roses in interesting containers from glazed pottery to a clear glass vase. Make an arrangement with a short, rounded bunch of tea roses in an old crock for the porch.

Preserving the Scents

When we mention the word "potpourri" most people think of roses. Tiny dried rosebuds mixed with rose petals and lavender makes a delightful potpourri. Pick petals when they are dry and at their blooming best. Cut off the heads and pull the petals off gently. You can mix them with dried herbs and geranium leaves.

To dry the roses, put a layer of petals in an airtight container and cover with salt. Add another layer and more salt and continue to layer in this way, stirring each time you add a new layer of petals. Add a pinch of cloves or allspice and cover tightly until ready to use. Then put it into a pretty basket or container.

Decorating with Roses

Rose-covered chintz with a white background is a lovely choice for slipcovers. In true English style your room will look as though the garden has come right indoors. Surprisingly, deep forest green on the leaves and stems with a variety of red and pink colors of roses is very easy to live with and to use with other colors and woods. It can look cheerful and refreshing with bare wood floors for spring and summer and comfortably sumptuous with an Oriental or Persian rug in cooler months. Add lots of greenery in a room with this fabric. Dark or light woods work well, as does painted furniture. A rose-covered fabric may seem busy but is actually quite calming and gives any room a well-dressed look.

Outdoor Living Room

If your roses are wandering over fences, creeping up the side of your house, even spilling onto the roof, take advantage of the backdrop and decorate your deck, patio, or lawn to blend right into the scenery. Soft, floppy pillows covered in rose fabric will add just the right touch to hard wooden, wicker, or metal outdoor furniture. In fact, they don't have to match. It doesn't take a lot of imagination to create an inviting outdoor spot for relaxing. Just toss an overstuffed cushion onto a chaise longue.

Nothing too ruffled, just a nice plump rosy pillow for dozing.

That Old-Fashioned Feeling

Give a new porch an old-fashioned feeling by placing two painted rocking chairs on either side of a nice old wicker or rugged wooden table. Fill the table with baskets or a pitcher of roses and wildflowers and add a soft cushion and a pretty throw pillow to each chair. Pink ticking or a plaid homespun is a nice choice of fabric.

SUMMER DECORATING

I recently received the new Laura Ashley Home catalog, which is a real treat. Laura Ashley fabrics have always represented country-inspired designs in the classic English tradition. This year's 152-page catalog is as much fun to browse through as an expensively produced coffee-table book. I often use their fabrics and wallpapers for my magazine features because they fit with all types of homes and are consistently well designed and easy to live with. Best of all, their products are moderately priced. Call 1-800-367-2000 to order.

This year's catalog provides all sorts of good ideas influenced by four distinctly different looks: English style; Mediterranean; American country; and, my favorite, Scandinavian simplicity. All seem to reflect a decorating trend toward simpler, more subtle, and uncluttered rooms. The direction in decorating is decidedly informality, comfort, and livability, which is perfect for the summer season.

No matter how finished our houses are, it's always compelling to redo with the change of seasons, especially when you go into the home furnishings stores or thumb through the new magazines. Here are some good tips I picked up that will help you create a fresh, up-to-date, and relaxing look for the summer months ahead.

Adding Colorful Accessories

If your rooms have been decorated in predominantly neutral colors and you're not ready for a total redo, add color through accessories and accent pieces. Simple additions like pillows for your sofa and chairs, new lampshades, vases, or collectibles will make the room look entirely different with very little effort.

Fresh Color Schemes

For summer, a blue-and-white scheme is always an instant hit and it never seems to look tired. But this year, the Scandinavian influence introduces accents of golden yellow with cornflower blue and it makes the tried-and-true look of blue and white more exciting and interesting. Hunter green with accents of yellow and white are also new this year and not just for fabrics, but for painted walls. Strong rich colors associated with classic English style include Laura Ashley's new brick and gold.

Small Rooms

Don't hesitate to use color in a small room, which will help maximize its coziness. For example, you can enhance the richness and warmth of a small den, library, or sitting room with deep color on the walls, windows, or upholstery, played off against dark wood furniture and crisp white accents. Bathrooms and powder rooms are also good candidates for using color.

Fabrics

This winter I discovered mattress ticking as a terrific fabric for making pillows, baby quilts, and seat cushions. It's also good looking when teamed with natural muslin for a lightweight quilted throw. The trick is to wash both the ticking and the muslin first to take away the sizing and make it really soft. Then I use the wrong side of the ticking fabric, which has a softer navy blue or a softer gray stripe than the right side of the fabric. You can create a whole new look from a classic material. I love muslin and prewashed sailcloth for pillows, slipcovers, quilts, and placemats. It never goes out of style and gets better looking with every washing.

Windows

Turn your windows into the room's focal point by choosing an intensely colored solid or print for the window treatments. Or, paint the trim a vibrant contrasting color, picking up one of the fabric colors in the room.

Walls

A whitewashed or sponged look is very popular for walls. If you can't afford a professional to do this, you should know there are lots of foolproof products on the market for doing the job yourself. An alternative is Laura Ashley's line of "Colorwash" wallpaper that actually reproduces a whitewashed effect on bright blue or coral-toned pink that looks like the real thing.

Furniture

Another great way to add color is by painting a piece of furniture in an unexpected color. A coat of paint in a vivid hue can transform furniture that may have seen better days, whether it's wood, metal, or wicker. If you don't already have something that can be made over with paint, scour flea markets or garage sales and you're sure to find a lively candidate.

Where to Begin

If you aren't sure about what color to use where, take inspiration from objects that appeal to you in the room. It might be a patchwork quilt, a rich tapestry wall hanging, a painting, a rug, or a fabric. Choose one of the least-used colors in your fabric to accentuate, and use it on walls, or around window trim, or in your accessories.

LIGHTEN UP, SUMMER'S HERE!

The other day I asked my favorite hair stylist if the onslaught of summer affects his business. "The first thing everyone does when the temperature changes is get 'summerized,'" he said. I thought this was a particularly succinct way to describe how we begin to edit our appearances for warm weather. Cutting one's hair and putting away winter clothing is what we do to get ourselves ready for summer. Summerizing our homes takes a bit more effort and storage space. Here are some tips for easy summerizing.

1. Roll up large rugs and leave floors bare or use scatter rugs here and there.
2. Clean out the basement and organize beach equipment in one area so it's handy and ready to go. I keep all kids' pails, shovels, etc., in a large Rubbermaid plastic laundry basket. We can put the whole thing in the car and hose it all down when we get home.
3. Make a space for beach towels. I put winter hats, gloves, and scarves in a plastic sweater box with cedar chips and use my hall closet shelf for beach towels and bags.
4. My friend Gretchen discovered large, quilted garment boxes with clear plastic zippered tops at Sears. They are perfect for holding blankets and winter clothes in the attic or closet. In the fall you can see what you've got.
5. I look for ways to lighten my furniture for summer. First I rearrange. This always gives me a lift. Then I try to eliminate some of it, which is always hard. Since we all live outdoors more in the summer you probably need less inside, if you have a place to store it.
6. Half-finished projects from winter probably won't get finished until fall. Face the facts and put it away. It's time for outdoor

living and there is no place in my house or time schedule for the reupholstery job I really did intend to finish by now. I live with the misguided opinion that if I trip over it enough I'll get to it. Not!

7. If you still have pine cones hanging around in baskets from last Christmas, put them away.

8. I've been faux-finishing all sorts of yard sale finds and now they're haphazardly hanging around after the fact. How many faux granite and marble plant holders can one really use, or for that matter display without seeming a bit fanatical? Each one isn't too bad looking, but all together it could be construed as having gone over the edge. Take a good look at your hobbies and knickknacks and put a few away for winter when you'll want to make a more cozy environment.

9. White paint is my all-purpose panacea. I walk around the house, brush and can in hand, touching up everything in sight. Paint the baseboards and door trims for an instant house-lift.

10. If you have draperies or heavy curtains, have them cleaned, pack them away, and replace them with sheer whites. I hung new white cafés over the kitchen sink and used a band of ecru eyelet for tiebacks.

11. Freshen the bedroom by covering the summer blanket or comforter with a crisp white sheet. It will make the bedroom look invitingly cool.

12. Sponge or spray-paint a large basket (even a laundry basket) and fill it with rolled-up guest towels. Add a fat ribbon bow to the handle and keep it on a small table or even on the floor if you're short of bathroom space. Organize all bathroom "stuff" in a pretty basket or ceramic bowl. The bathroom will seem instantly fresher.

13. Plan a yard sale and place the ad. This will give you a target date to clean out everything you don't need. Price it all to go!

14. My friend Nancy and her daughter Sam blame me for all their half-finished projects because I gave them one of my books of decorating tips. My advice: In the summertime, don't take on any project that takes more than fifteen minutes. It's summer, remember?

15. Another friend got carried away with spring energy and pulled out a huge bush that now sits waiting to be carted away. Lesson: Take care of one project or trouble spot that bothers you, then relax and enjoy the summer. You'll feel you deserve it.

COZY MAKEOVERS FOR WINTER

As winter approaches, everyone I meet is working on or thinking about starting a creative project. It might be making a quilt, or spending a lot of time cooking, or learning to play an instrument. In fact, most people will tell you they have so many things they want to do during the winter that they don't know where to start. How does this warm up our homes for winter?

Making our homes an inviting place to be has more to do with what goes on there than how it looks. The big word of advice to come down in the nineties from the decorators on high is "comfort." When asked, "What is the most important ingredient to consider when designing a room?" there is no hesitation among the professionals. If you can't plunk yourself down with the Sunday papers and enjoy a cup of coffee with your feet up, no amount of prettiness matters.

Creating a Comfort Zone

If you can make your home a real comfort zone you won't tend to feel closed in as the days get colder and shorter. In fact, your home should be the place you most want to be, not the place you want to leave. This can be achieved easily by answering the following questions.

Q. What do I most enjoy doing in my leisure time at home?

A. If you don't have the perfect spot to do this, think about what it would take to create such an area in your home. If, for example, you're a quilter but don't have a proper sewing room (who does?), perhaps you can make a place for it in a corner of the living room. You might not use the living room for crafting during the rest of the year, and feel it messes up the space, but having an ongoing project in the winter can make the place look cozy and interesting, and best of all it's always set up and accessible so you're drawn to it. Organize the material so it works for you. Even if you do more than one thing, find places for all your projects so you can do one thing here and another there, depending on your mood, and not have to put it away every day.

Q. Is there a new indoor skill, hobby, craft, etc., I'd like to learn?

A. Before taking up a new hobby, create a place to do it where you'll be totally encouraged not to drop it for lack of comfortable space.

Q. How do I most like to entertain friends?

A. Entertaining is often more intimate in the winter. Change your style. If you usually had friends for dinner in the summer, you might consider Sunday brunch in the kitchen. Or make the perfect cozy place for afternoon coffee by the fire with a friend. Buy a really great teapot. Cover your dining table with a quilt. Use warm colors to set your table.

Q. In what room am I most comfortable?

A. Articulate exactly what makes your favorite room the most comfortable. If its possible, improve on this for winter. Take some of this comfort and apply it to other rooms.

Q. What part of the house do I tend to avoid?

A. Why do you avoid this room? Take stock and try to figure out a way to get maximum use from this room. The furniture may need to be rearranged, or you may need to come up with an entirely new use for the room. Sometimes low lighting does the trick. Or, if it's dark, add a lamp or two.

Q. Where and at what time of day does the sun come in the most?

A. For me, making the most of the sun is of optimum importance. Place your desk, for example, in a sunny window. Or create a table and chairs for breakfast in the most sunny spot. When the sun fills a particular room, what activities are you doing in the house? Try to switch the place you do it to the sunny spot so you don't miss those warm feelings for part of the day. If you work all day, this might be something you can' achieve only on weekends. Make the most of it.

Q. Am I basically a neat, organized person, or do I like to spread my things about in a more haphazard manner?

A. This is not a judgment call. When you ask someone if they are neat and organized they tend to get defensive. If you feel better in disarray, don't fight it. Work with it to your advantage. In the winter it's comforting to have more "stuff" around. Organize the areas that bother you most.

Q. If you live with others, do you have a spot in the house that's just for yourself?

A. Having a place that's your very own is important, especially if you have small children. Find that place and be firm about it being your "selfish spot."

Q. What bothers you the most about your home?

A. Really look hard at what bothers you about your home and ask if there is anything you can do about it. My nemesis is no dining room. I can't add one on right now so I keep changing where the dining table resides. It helps for awhile and then I change it again. Do what you can to improve what you don't like, or at least minimize its discomfort.

Q. What do you like the most?

A. Don't mess with a good thing. Whatever works, use to your advantage. Play it up.

Q. If you could change one thing, what would it be?

A. If you don't know what you'd like to do in your leisure time this winter, why not work on the one thing you'd change that you don't like about your house. If it's something that's unchangeable, or that you can't afford to do, work on a small aspect of it. Make a two- or three-stage plan and begin to set the ground work. You might find a creative solution that you didn't know was there all along. And, finally, make the most of winter. It doesn't last that long.

WARMING UP FOR WINTER

When the weather outside begins to turn chilly it's time to make your indoor environment as warm and cozy as possible. There are many small things you can do to achieve this.

Small Touches to Warm Your Home

A friend had a dinner party for six friends on an especially cold evening. Her centerpiece was a stroke of genius, thought up on the spot as she shopped for the food in her local supermarket. There she bought little pots of primroses and arranged them in the center of the table, leaving them in the white paper surrounding each one. Upon leaving the party each guest was given one of the little plants. As they went out into the snowy, freezing night, the sight of the little flowering plants almost made you think it was spring.

This week I filled the house with tulips, freesia, and a basket filled with white primrose pots. It's a small extravagance in the middle of winter to have fresh cut flowers all around. This is a great antidote to the weather and a quick and easy spirit enhancer.

It doesn't take much to warm the look of your home during frigid days. Here are a few ideas.

Sparkle in the Night

Some people keep those tiny clear Christmas tree lights up all year long. I am reluctant to take them down. The tiny lights wrap around bare tree branches that are quite sculptural and when it's dark outside it adds a festive sparkle. It would be just as good to have in an entryway in your house when you want a little light but not too much brightness. Consider wrapping a ficus tree, for example. Another string of lights outlines the inside of my glass-front china cabinet. It makes glasses and vases twinkle and adds a nice soft lighting to this area.

Fresh as Spring

Start a pot of bulbs in the house. Paper whites are so fresh and sweetly scented. Line several pots on a windowsill, or clear a bookshelf and put them there. I like to put the clay pots holding these plants everywhere—on the kitchen counter, on a coffee table, or  on a plant stand in a corner of the living room. The bulbs bloom incredibly fast and make you think spring can't be too far away.

Greenery

When the snow is falling outside I especially like to have leafy green plants inside. The snow is a wonderful backdrop. Put a small table in front of a window and group plants on top to catch the sunlight. This will give your room a fresh lift.

Family Photos

This is a good time of year to sort out your snapshots. Cut and frame your favorites and group them on a tabletop, or mat and frame them for hanging on a wall. Select an area that seems appropriate, such as a hallway, or a narrow wall in the bedroom, and arrange photographs that go together. When we stay indoors a lot we often like to surround ourselves with collections, favorite comfortable items, and more things than we like to have around in warm weather.

The Charm of Handmade Items

Even though I have a down comforter on my bed, I took out a handmade crocheted white afghan to fold on the end of the bed. It makes the room cozier and gives the bed texture.

Candlelight

This is a good time to polish silver and brass candlesticks if you have them. Use white or ivory candles and group them for candlelight dinners. I have candles everywhere and light them often as the sun goes down. Somehow it helps me accept the shorter days.

Getting Ahead

Use time spent in the house on the weekend to wash, bleach, and starch tired kitchen curtains. I did this over the weekend. I hadn't intended to, but one curtain sort of led to another and when I rehung them it gave my kitchen an instant lift. Everything looked so cheerful that I ironed lace-edged linen napkins to use, on the diagonal, for valances. There is something cleansing about seeing crisp white curtains against the background of a snowy yard.

Little Things Mean a Lot

There are little things that don't take much money or time that we can do to make our homes more enjoyable for the long winter days. Sorting out an underwear drawer can be done while watching TV and, while a small thing to do, it can make you feel enormously organized. Arrange a vase filled with flowers for your bedroom. Add lace-edged pillow shams to the bed. When I can't afford to buy a set of Ralph Lauren sheets, I buy lace-edged pillow cases as consolation. It perks up the bedroom and my sense of well-being.

Fix It Now

Finally, it's time to fix that particular thing that drives you crazy. Why wait until you have more important things to do outside. Get it over with so you can enjoy knowing that you did it and stop saying, "One of these days I have to do . . ." Why not today?

WINTER CRAFTING

Did you know that 90 percent of U.S. households have at least one family member engaged in a craft or hobby? The breakdown is: Most people make things to give as gifts, followed by making things for personal use, next for home decorating, followed by holiday decorations, and finally to sell. I was surprised to learn that the craft with the greatest growth interest is wreath-making, followed by cross stitch/embroidery. These figures come from the Hobby Industry Association. March is National Craft Month, celebrating the contributions that crafts make to traditions around the world. While countless generations continue to pass on time-honored skills such as quilting, knitting, needlepoint, floral arranging, and sewing, many contemporary crafters also share information about the newest tools and techniques, such as glue guns and rub-on stencils, to make crafting quicker and easier.

In keeping with this, stores across the country, such as Michael's craft stores and JoAnn's or Cloth World fabric stores, run special sales, tie-ins, classes, and demonstrations. If you are interested in learning a new craft, the wintertime is a good time to plan it. Call the craft and hobby supply stores and sewing centers in your area for more information.

Freshen Up with Pillows

Give your sofa and living room chairs a fresh look with new pillows. They are easy to make and it can be fun to combine fabric remnants. If you travel, take advantage of the fact that fabric stores tend to reflect the climate and mood of their locale. You'll almost always find something new and unusual that can add excitement to your home. While in Key West, Florida, I was attracted to the vibrant tropical colors and made pillows from bright fuchsia, turquoise, and yellow. I also love the Bali prints. These prints and colors will look different from anything I could find at home on Nantucket.

Tablecovers

Tablecloths, napkins, and placemats are easy sewing projects and will give you a chance to use up remnants. Make each napkin from a different fabric. Create a patchwork of squares from which to cut a tablecloth. I used a pale, rose-printed Laura Ashley fabric to make a tablecloth for my outdoor dining table because it will go with the roses that are planted in my garden and that climb up my fence. If you have a garden, look for fabrics in colors to match your flowers. You'll be happy you did this before the garden beckons you outdoors.

Painted Wooden Accessories

If you visit a craft outlet you'll surely come home with a bag full of crafting material you never intended to buy. It's amazing when you find things that you never knew you *had* to have. There are all sorts of wooden accessories from tree ornaments to wooden stools, trays, and boxes. These items are fun to paint.

Make a Baby Quilt

Baby quilts are fun and easy to make with just 2 yards of fabric. Using two contrasting prints, or a print and a solid, cut 15 squares, each 6 1/2 inches, from each fabric print. Alternating the squares, stitch 6 rows of 5 squares each. Then, create a patchwork pattern of the alternating rows and stitch them together. Use one of the fabrics or a coordinating color for the backing and cut it 1 1/2 inches larger than the front all around. Pin the backing, batting, and patchwork front together and quilt 1/4 inch in from each side of all seam lines. Draw diagonal lines to form an *X* in each of the patchwork squares and quilt along these lines. When finished, bring the extra

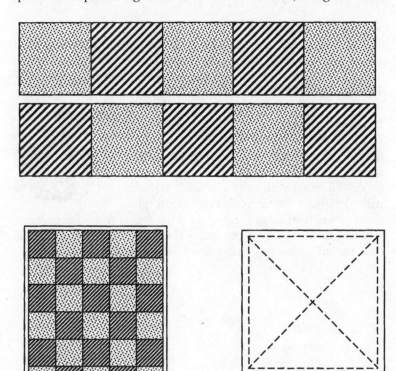

backing fabric to the front, fold over the raw edge onto the front of the finished quilt, and slipstitch or machine stitch all around.

Faux Furniture

If you've ever yearned to own a faux-painted piece of furniture, you might like to know that it's easier than you think to create your own. Craft stores and home centers carry a variety of faux finishing kits and decorative touches in aerosol cans for easy-to-do finishes like marbleizing, sponging, and glazing. Formby's Decorative Touches products now include premixed glaze in light, medium, and dark with foolproof directions. You simply paint the furniture with any waterbase paint, then mix equal parts of that paint with the glaze, and apply it to the furniture with a sponge, combing squeegee, or rag. The effects are dynamite. I've done it with lots of pieces and I'm always amazed at how good they look.

Wreath Making

Start way ahead of the season and make lots of Christmas ornaments and a wreath from dried materials. All the fixings—from beads to dried flowers to pine cones to bells, buttons, and bows—are found in craft stores. And, if you've never used a hot glue gun you're in for a surprise. It makes crafting a cinch. These tools come in small, hobby sizes and all you do is add a spot of glue wherever you want to adhere something, and presto! It's done. No waiting to dry. If you're making a wreath covered with delightful decorations you simply glue  them where you want them. And don't forget to add a gorgeous bow made from one of the many French-wired ribbons you can buy pretied, or by the yard. Glue it on as well.

# WINTERIZING

European cities like Paris and Barcelona offer one of the most wonderful perks: public places to people-watch. It's so civilized and entertaining to have a cup of coffee or eat lunch at a sidewalk café. These public places provide an environment for casual meetings without the pressure to entertain at home. The earliest watering holes were probably the first versions of the neighborhood café or diner. In many small towns like mine, we have public benches on Main Street. People often stroll into town on the weekends or on a summer night and sit on a bench and chat. Almost every other person is someone you know. This small gesture reinforces our sense of community.

Expanding Inward

Going into winter we have to think about this connection in a different way. In that regard our homes become the center of our universe, the place where we spend much of our leisure time. Making our homes more inviting and cozy is a goal we often try to achieve with the onset of shorter days. Many of us love any excuse to fix up, redo, change our interior design, collect and arrange things, cook a good meal, learn a new hobby, and share an evening at home with friends. In short, our homes become our comfort zones.

Arrange Furniture for Your Needs

There are many ways to arrange your furnishings for relating in different ways. Some of us need a place to curl up with a book and be totally private. We may need a place to enjoy a cup of tea with a friend. An intimate dinner for six requires a different sort of space as does a casual Sunday brunch in the kitchen. As your outdoor activities begin to shut down, take stock of your home. You may have been entertaining and living outdoors on the deck or patio all summer so you haven't yet thought about the switch to indoor living. Think about the way you live—or would like to live—and reevaluate your rooms with this in mind.

New and Affordable Ideas

Arranging furniture for different situations is one thing, but what if you're tired of what you have? There are many new trends on the horizon that don't cost a great deal.

1. One of the newer decorating ideas is to use outdoor furniture indoors, with one twist. Adding softness, such as a cushion or a slipcover to wrought iron or teak furniture gives it a supple, warm look.
2. Many of the better-known decorators are using office furniture in living and dining rooms as well. Here, too, you can add a fabric cushion to soften the sleek lines, but the result is carefree and unusual, if that's what you're after. Office furniture is often easy to find through catalogs or buy used. Spray paint, and faux finishes like Formby's Decorative Touches in granite or marble can do wonders to turn a dull gray metal desk into a dynamite piece. Sofas made for offices and lobbies, for example, are sturdy and carefree, with few loose cushions. These can be good looking and perfect for homes with small children. If you think this sort of furniture looks institutional, you're in for a surprise. Look through the shelter magazines. You'll often find an eclectic mix of sleek office chairs around a country, pine dining table.
3. If you yearn for really good furniture but can't afford it right now, elegant fabric goes a long way toward achieving the look you want. A brocade tablecloth can cover an old dining table. Throw pillows made with vintage fabrics or satin covers are sensational. I have them on a sofa that desperately needs new slipcovers, and it was instantly updated to modern status.
4. There are imaginative ways to furnish your home with found objects. Years ago I spent a lot of time at a salvage yard in Connecticut. I never dreamed those odd artifacts and "junk" taken from crumbling buildings would have so much appeal for today's decorators.

However you define your living space or add to its interest, no matter what new trends are introduced or how we integrate our work in our homes, it's good to remember that comfort is never out of style.

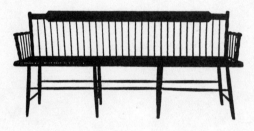

Temporary
Quarters

PERSONALIZING A RENTAL

"How can I make my rented apartment personal without spending any money on major changes?" I hear this from many newlyweds as well as people who rent vacation homes. My husband and I take our work with us to a house we rent in Key West, Florida, for two months in the winter. I've found that it's important to do whatever I can to make the house seem like home in the first couple of days, before I begin to settle in.

Outdoor Dining

Dress up plastic or wrought iron deck chairs with no-sew cushions. Simply wrap foam rubber, cut to size, with pretty fabric and tie ribbon bows on the corners to hold the fabric in place.

Instant Landscaping

Rush to the local garden center and buy a bunch of flowering plants in terra-cotta pots to place around the deck, patio, or sitting area in the yard. A small basket filled with impatiens or geraniums will set off the breakfast table.

Cover-Up

Any old, ugly, or just plain boring sofa or chair can be livened up with throw pillows and a quilt. Use the quilt to cover the sofa, or use a pretty sheet for an instant slipcover. Just drape it and tuck everywhere. Then add the throw pillows to match.

Clean Livin'

If your rental came furnished and has lots of the owner's belongings around, clear them away. Store all the tabletop knickknacks away in a box. Use pitchers, vases, and other interesting containers to hold small arrangements of flowers. If you don't like the paintings on the walls, remove them. Put up something of your own.

Small Personal Touches Make a Big Difference

Having your own things around makes a space feel like your own. I always have piles of books on a chair or ottoman and framed family pictures to fill a living room tabletop. A quilt on the bed or over the sofa for cold nights—or even hanging on the wall—can warm up an impersonal environment.

Rearranging Things

The arrangement of furniture might not be to your liking. Rearrange it to make the layout more comfortable for your use of each room. Create your spot for whatever it is you do when relaxing, and outfit it with your personal treasures. Make the traffic flow for your needs.

Lighten Up for Summer

If the house is dark, you might be able to roll up and store carpets away. Heavy drapes can be removed and replaced with inexpensive sheer panels or cafés. Cut flowers in vases brighten every room. Tie back curtain panels with ribbons.

Small Additions for Big Results

If the house is a bit cold and barren it's easy to make it warm and charming. Cover bare wooden furniture, such as a dining table, with a patchwork quilt. Put runners on a sideboard or end table. Inexpensive rag rugs are good solutions for bare floors. In the bathroom, use interesting containers to hold personal essentials on the countertop. Fill a mantelpiece with your own collectibles. Pots of fresh herb plants smell great and are practical in a basket on a kitchen counter.

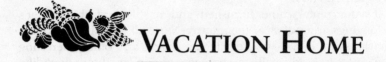

VACATION HOME

Decorating a vacation home can be a lot of fun. You don't have to adhere to any rules and nothing you buy has to be too precious, expensive, or lasting. You can feel free to experiment with ideas. Most of all, whatever you select in the way of furniture, fabrics, or wall and floor coverings should be designed for easy care.

Getting Organized

Vacation homes call for a different kind of organization. You want everything to be carefree so you can enjoy your leisure time. There shouldn't be any knickknacks around that require dusting and care. The furniture should be weather resistant and, when possible, the fabric you choose should be treated for indoor/outdoor use.

Weekend Guests

Being organized is the key to a successful weekend with guests afoot. Make your home an oasis rather than a three-ring circus. Having guests requires three make-ready plans:

1. Shopping for food and planning meals.
2. Planning activities, or at least knowing what events are going on that might be of interest to your guests.
3. Making sure transportation is provided.

Take Stock of Your Environment

If you usually have guests in the summertime, use the middle of winter or early spring when you have a few minutes here and there to fuss with things that need painting, sewing, recovering, or making. Take stock. Fix, repair, or spruce up what you know will bother you later if it isn't done, and make the time to do it beforehand.

Romance with Candlelight

Create a romantic tabletop with lots of candles in interesting candle holders. There are many different kinds at all different prices, but this is one area that won't cost much to make an impact. For an elegant but casual table setting, use delicate wrought iron candlesticks to hold fat and thin candles. Hurricane lamps are exquisite and would be perfect on a patio table all summer long. Or group a bunch of interesting votive holders for a centerpiece.

Light and Airy

Woven placemats and napkins in natural colors are classic. They never go out of style and always look refreshingly new. Add a small votive candle at each person's place above the placemat.

Seashore Dinner

Set the table with pure white candles set into fat glasses, or clear vases in which flowers are delivered from the florist. You can find them for pennies at a thrift shop or Salvation Army. Next, add Queen Anne's lace, chicory, or thistle for a casual floral arrangement. Place small white votives, each in a shell, around the flowers. Sprinkle a variety of shells on the table between each placesetting.

Fix-All

QUICK FURNITURE FIXES

Yard sales and auctions are good places to find unusual pieces of furniture, among other things. Most furniture you find, however, is usually in need of minor and sometimes major repair. Before taking it home, be sure you're confident that you can fix whatever needs fixing and that the item won't end up at *your* next sale.

Scratches

To quickly conceal minor scratches on cherry, maple, or mahogany, use mercurochrome or iodine. Use liquid shoe polish in a color to match walnut or oak.

If there's a deep scratch, it can be touched up with stain. Then fill the cavity with polyurethane. Let dry and sand lightly with extra-fine sandpaper. Go over the area, and the entire surface if needed, with paste wax such as Butcher's or Johnson's.

Gouges

Plastic wood can be used to fill deep gouges. If the gouges are shallow they can easily be sanded and restained.

White Marks

Water rings don't have to be permanent. It's easy to remove them with a mixture of toothpaste and baking soda. If the white ring was caused by heat, rub with a cloth and mayonnaise. Wipe, let dry, then rub with furniture oil.

Burns

Use a Q-Tip dipped in nail polish remover to rub the darkened area. Take care not to touch the surrounding surface. Mix equal parts of nail polish remover and clear nail polish and dab with the brush over the scarred area.

REMODELING TIPS: PROS, CONS, SOLUTIONS

If only home decorating were as simple as buying a bed! When you purchase a new bed you can go to a showroom and try every mattress in the place. You can turn, squirm, and bounce. But you can't do this when deciding whether to carpet or put down wood floors. You can't really know how the paint will look before you've put brush to wall. So what's the good news and the bad when it comes to remodeling?

Wood Flooring

The good news is plain and simple: Hardwood floors look great. They add character to your rooms like nothing else can. The bad news is that wood won't absorb sound. The solution is to use overstuffed furniture, area carpets, and curtains or drapes in rooms with wood floors.

Care and Repair

The good news: Several coats of polyurethane over new wood should protect it from spills, scratches, and everyday traffic. The bad news is that it can be cold. Even if you love bare floors, you may want to carpet the bedrooms.

In the Scheme of Things

Wood floors go with any decorating style; and you can use any color fabric, area carpet, or paint with it. The bad news: A floor finish won't last forever. The National Wood Flooring Association recommends recoating the wood every three to five years.

High Ceilings

Many remodelers remove ceilings to the rafters or build additions with cathedral ceilings for a spacious, contemporary feeling. The good news is that the room or house will appear larger than it is because you feel more space above you; your eye tends to go up. Angled ceilings are also desirable for added drama. The bad news is, heat rises, so high ceilings are impractical in cold climates. One solution is to install ceiling fans to circulate the air.

Luxury Bathroom

When their last child left home, a couple I know did something just for themselves. They converted their daughter's bedroom into a luxurious bathroom. While it was a small bedroom, it was a wonderfully spacious bathroom complete with whirlpool bathtub, marble tiles, oversized shower, built-in TV, and exercise equipment. The good news is, if the room already exists, you don't incur the expense of adding on a room. The bad news is, if the room isn't near existing plumbing, the transformation could be costly. However, this is a project that can be done for a little or a lot depending on the materials used and how far you want to go.

Let There Be Light

When we converted an attic space we installed a skylight in the sloped roof. The good news: This is the most efficient way to get natural light into a room. If you have an older home, consider this when doing a remodeling project. The bad news: We installed a skylight over our bed and the sun or moon often interrupts our sleep. Skylights can be cold in winter and hot in summer. Solution: look into operable skylights that let heat escape and roll-up screens to block the sun.

Window Wonders

Installing large expanses of windows or a wall of French doors with lots of glass panes can be wonderful for letting light in, but at night they create big black areas. Solution: Consider the type of window treatments that will work for day and night.

You want to expose as much of the window as possible during the day and easily close out the night when you want warmth and privacy.

Kitchen Krazy

"My kitchen is driving me crazy," is a common complaint. Nobody ever thinks they have enough room or the right kind of space. Kitchens are the most often renovated room in the house. Many people want big open kitchen family room combinations for informal meals and for watching small children at play. That's the good news. The bad news: The sounds of pots and pans often fight with the television noise and conversations going on in the family room. Appliances can seem positively thunderous when you sit down for a quiet evening in the family room. Solution: whisper-soft appliances and folding doors between rooms.

 # HANG IT UP

You've just moved into your first home and haven't gotten around to buying tools. You've arranged the furniture and now you want to hang a few pictures on the wall. You go to your local hardware store only to discover there are thousands of little items made for hanging all sorts of things on the wall. How do you decide what to buy? The answer is more in where you want to hang it.

What's in a Wall?

The best way to hang anything is on a wall stud, but these can be impossible to locate. To hang pictures on drywalls, which is what you find in today's homes, there are three basic anchors that can be used. The weight of the object to be hung should be considered since each anchor has different weight-bearing capacity. You'll need a drill, a hammer, and a screwdriver for each of the following:

Jack Nut

(A small molly bolt.) Use this on hollow doors to support light weights. Drill a hole through one side of the door, and the jack nut, with a removable screw, is tapped into place.

Molly Bolt

This can be used on drywall board. Drill a hole and tap this bolt into place. Then tighten the screw. A collapsible flange will expand behind the drywall as it is tightened. Be careful not to overtighten. Once it is firm, remove the 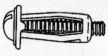 screw. Molly bolts do not work on masonry walls or plaster.

Toggle Bolts

Use this for plaster walls. It has spring-loaded wings that flair open when inserted through a previously drilled hole. Once in place it can never be removed because the wings will drop inside the wall when the screw is removed. At Builder's Square, the hardware expert said that whatever will be fastened by the toggle bolt must be connected to the anchor before it is inserted into the wall.

Teflon Tip

There's a variety of bolts with Teflon tips. They requires only a hammer and a screwdriver and look similar to a Molly bolt, but the end of the screw is pointed like a nail, and covered with Teflon. You decide where 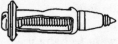 you want the picture, then nail it through the drywall. The Teflon allows the support to drive through the drywall. Then you tighten the screw until the metal flange expands on the back of the wall, and retract the screw.

# PAINTING KNOW-HOW

The most common do-it-yourself job for both men and women is painting. A friend of mine likes to paint everything white and every spring she gives all her furniture a new coat of white paint. This year she's redoing her kitchen. She doesn't care if the job is done neatly, only that it gets done. However, if you'd rather do it right the first time, here are some tips from paint expert Jeff Steenburgen at Builder's Square.

Selecting Paint

Shop for quality. Cheaper paints tend not to adhere as well as good-quality paints. The result is that you may have to apply an extra coat to get the coverage you want, which will end up costing as much as or more than a better brand.

Getting Ready

Take everything off the walls and put your furniture in the middle of the room. Don't scrimp on plastic drop cloth to cover your possessions. It tends to tear when spread out. Use a plastic cover of one millimeter that's tough enough to stretch and shed paint droplets.

Prepare the Surface

Preparation includes sanding and priming. You shouldn't have any glossy surfaces. The shiny areas should be roughed up with sandpaper to ensure proper adhesion of the new paint. Also, old paint should be thoroughly scraped so that all loose chips are knocked free of the surface, otherwise the loose chip will break off with the fresh paint.

Get Tough

Toughen and smooth the rough areas. Sometimes drywalls have small cracks and holes, including the holes made by picture hooks. Fill them with putty or spackle. Let it dry, then sand it smooth.

Clean Up

Vacuum the room before painting so the dust you stir up won't settle on the wet paint. Wipe the walls as well and scrub surfaces to be painted.

Mask It Out

Mask windows, doors, and other areas you won't be painting. Now's the time to use the thinner plastic. It can be cut to size and taped to cover windows and doors. Or you can use newspaper for this.

Take Time to Prime

Use a proper primer for unfinished wood, drywall, or plaster. The thin primer coat helps the finished coat adhere to the surface. Always prime any latex surface that is to be covered with oil-based paint. If you are making a significant color change, then a white primer coat will help cover the old color.

Paneling

Don't paint over finished interior paneling. The high gloss will repel the paint, and cheaper grades of paneling will buckle and disintegrate from wet paint.

CHEAP FIX-UP IDEAS

Did you know that Americans spend 1.5 hours every day on do-it-yourself projects? In a recent survey reported in *American Demographics,* overall, home improvement projects ranked fourth among day-to-day leisure activities. Number one is watching TV, then socializing, and third, reading.

Saving by Doing It Yourself

Fortunately you don't have to spend a lot of money to give your home a new look. In fact, according to home improvement statistics, you can make some dramatic changes in and outside your home for under $25. Here are a few suggestions:

1. Philips Lighting Company makes three light bulbs in their IQ Lighting Series: The Dimmer has a built-in computer chip so you can select up to four light levels without special fixtures; the Auto Off turns itself off after thirty minutes; and the Back-Up has a secondary filament that remains on after the main filament burns out. All bulbs are $4.99 each.
2. Earth Light Collection makes compact fluorescent light bulbs designed to replace incandescent bulbs for energy savings. They cost $20 per lamp.
3. Stenciling is less expensive than painting or wallpapering, it can change the look of a room in less time and for less money. Average cost for a stenciling set is $9.
4. Installing new fixtures is a quick and easy way to accent a room. In the bathroom, for example, practical additions like a long towel bar (I use wooden dowels and brass boating fixtures), large brass hooks for hanging a robe, or new cabinet knobs can alter the entire look of the room. Prices range from $3 to $12.
5. Faux finishing with a ragging technique is easy and fun. All you need are two paint colors and a bunch of rags. You paint the

light color on first and dab the darker color over it with a pouncing and rolling motion in an overall, irregular manner.

6. Is storage space a problem? Adding a shelf in a closet or pantry is a great way to gain space. We've recycled lots of great pieces of wood, or you can buy metal or wire shelves in the sizes needed. All brackets and screws come with them at home centers. Average cost of a shelf is $20.

7. Window boxes filled with seasonal flowers will give the front of your house a facelift.

8. A little paint goes a long way. Painting all the window trim on your house will make a world of difference. Once you decide that everything doesn't have to be done in a heartbeat, you're free to put in that statistically correct 1.5 hours a day on your home, with plenty of time left over for summer fun.

TOOLS FOR QUICK FIX-UPS

If you've just moved into your first home you may not realize that the first thing you'll need is some basic tools for simple around-the-house tasks. This may not sound very exciting, but before you turn around something will need fixing. Most of us, even those who have been homeowners for a long time, never seem to have the right tools in the right place when we need them. I spoke to a knowledgeable person at Builder's Square who advised outfitting a toolbox with practical necessities for simple repairs and then adding specialty items as you come up against a job requiring them.

The Basic Toolbox

The I-mean-business look of those green metal toolboxes are at first appealing, until you think about lifting them filled with tools. Go for the inexpensive plastic 19-inch model with a tray at the top. The lift-out tray allows you to take only the tools you need to the place where you need them. The cost is around $8.

What Goes In It

1. You don't need a whole bunch of different size hammers. For around $10 you can buy a 16-ounce claw, which is the one with a curved end for pulling nails. This is perfect for pounding in picture hooks and making simple repairs.
2. Add a few nails and screws in common sizes.
3. A staple gun for about $13 is really handy when you want to tack up Christmas lights, tack down carpets, and do simple upholstery jobs.
4. My all-time favorite tool is a hot glue gun. I use it for craft projects as well as for fixing screws permanently in place and tacking decorative trim onto any surface.
5. A toolbox-sized short-cut saw, which costs about $12, will take care of simple trim work like cutting down a Christmas tree, trimming branches, or making picture frames.
6. A hack saw is needed for cutting metal and costs around $8. A couple of extra blades are $2. Get them at the same time and you'll be grateful at some point.
7. A utility knife is a necessity for opening boxes and trimming wallpaper or cutting twine. The blades come inside. A heavy metal model will hold up better than a lightweight plastic knife.
8. An adjustable wrench is perfect for opening stuck screw tops and assembling furniture and toys. Try them out so you get one that fits your hand comfortably. A channel lock wrench will let you get more twisting power.
9. Slip joint pliers cost about $5 and are indispensable for pulling out staples, small nails, picture hooks, and such.
10. You'll need a set of screwdrivers. They start at $10 and go up. This is something you can't do without, and having just one screwdriver won't do. You need both Phillips head (the cross-shaped model) and flat head or slot screwdrivers. At one time or another you'll need everything from the tiny eyeglass size to a hefty 1/4-inch flat head.
11. A power screwdriver is something that, once you own it, you'll wonder how you ever got along without it. Stanley tools makes one that is lightweight, easy to use, and durable. If you have arthritis or limited hand strength, this is a must.
12. A cordless power drill with a set of extra drill bits is another good item.

13. Wire cutters round out the basic hand tool inventory. Purchase a 4- or 5-inch model for about $8.

14. A roll of black plastic electrical tape is essential for emergency repairs on hoses and temporary fixes on faulty appliances in a pinch.

15. A roll of duct tape is a necessity for any home.

16. If you want to be completely set, add a $4 electrical circuit tester so you'll know for sure if the electricity has been cut off when you decide to fix a wall plug, switch, or socket. A pair of safety glasses for $12 is another little insurance item.

17. A 12-foot tape measure, which costs around $8, and a level for hanging curtain rods and pictures on the wall will come in very handy. You'll be quite satisfied when you get pictures hung right the first time rather than trying to eyeball it.

18. One last item that won't fit in the toolbox, but that you'll one day thank yourself for getting before you needed it, is a plunger. They're not expensive, but can save you hours of grief or embarrassment should you need one when guests are visiting.

Now that you're all tooled up, you might want to know about something else for doing it yourself. A company called Books That Work publishes multimedia software with home and garden titles. Their newest release is *Home Repair Encyclopedia*. It's a comprehensive reference tool that provides step-by-step instructions for more than one hundred home projects and is available on CD-ROM for Windows at retail computer and software stores nationwide for around $30. It calculates everything from energy and lumber cost, to the materials needed for a wallpaper or tiling project. You have to have an IBM PC or 100 percent compatible, 386 or higher, 2MB RAM minimum; VGA or Super VGA monitor and Windows 3.1. If you want more information, contact Books That Work, 2300 Geng Road, Bldg. 3, Suite 100, Palo Alto, CA 94303, or phone (800) 242–4546.

Holiday
Decorating

HOLIDAY ENTERTAINING

The invitation read, "Please come celebrate the holidays with Christmas cheer and lite bite."

It turned out to be the best party I've attended in years, which is what got me thinking about this subject. What does it take to have a really great party? It doesn't just happen without a lot of planning and a conscious effort on someone's part. But the key is that it should appear to have happened with the greatest of ease.

'Tis the season to be fêted and to fête. Beginning with setting the stage and ending with the mix of people, the following ingredients went into that terrific party I'm talking about, and you can take it from there.

1. The house was perfectly set up for the festivities. Lights blinking along the driveway fence put us in a holiday mood before we ever reached the house, and even made the rainy night less dreary.
2. Candlelight and low lighting made everything and everyone look like an airbrushed photo. No apparent flaws. Don't skimp on candles. Put votives along mantels, on bookcases, in niches, as well as grouped on tables. Surround them with greens.
3. The furniture in each room was arranged for easy flow from food to drinks to places to sit and balance plates or drinks.
4. At one end of the buffet table was a basket filled with green napkins tied with red ribbons and holding silverware.
5. Every room, even those not used, was softly lit and there was the subtlest of decoration in each—a lampshade entwined with

a wreath of silver and gold stars, the Christmas tree, of course, and holiday greenery.

6. So much for setting the stage. Now for the star of the evening. The food was sensational. Not just good, not just great, but at the risk of using an overworked word, it was awesome. The presentation was simple and ungimmicky. And different types of dishes were placed in two locations with plates of Christmas cookies here and there. The mixture of fish, meat, cheese, and vegetable dishes was perfectly balanced for all tastes. There was finger food and plate food, giving everyone the opportunity to sit, or to stand and mingle. And trays of tidbits were passed often but not intrusively.

7. Separating the food from the bar kept people moving through the house rather than having them gather around one table. This party was catered, so the host and hostess were free to enjoy their guests and to remain gracious and relaxed. I realize not everyone can have a catered affair, but you can plan ahead for a smooth party. Once that first guest arrives, the partygivers should be hassle free to enjoy what they've created. If you are uptight and racing nervously about, everyone feels uncomfortable.

8. And finally, the guest list. The holidays are a good time to invite everyone you know to drop by. But a selective guest list that includes those with similar interests, or close friends and relatives, or a mix of different ages, or the people you work with, can also determine the ambience of a party. It's also fun to mix old and close friends with friends that are new, or to invite an acquaintance from out of town or from another country.

Party Ideas

The following are a few ideas for a party theme or for decorating your home for partygiving.

1. My daughter Robby went to a Sunday afternoon dessert party. Everyone was required to bring three dozen baked cookies, all the same. The hostess had prepared tins for all the guests and everyone exchanged cookies and filled tins so each person went home with a mixed batch of Christmas cookies. This is a good party for young families with children.

2. For a dramatic effect, decorate with only one color such as red or silver or white. For example, tie a bunch of winterberry branches with a red bow on the door, set the table with a red

cloth or shiny paper and use plaid or white napkins tied with red yarn or ribbons. Use pots of poinsettias everywhere, and red tulips or amaryllis for the centerpiece with lots of red candles at various heights.

3. As a centerpiece, fill a clear glass bowl with red tree balls. For a sitdown dinner, set the table with white plates and place a small red package wrapped with white satin ribbon at each placesetting. Hollow out a hole in the top of shiny apples and insert a small candle. Place one in front of each plate.

4. Stencil gold stars on terra-cotta pots, fill them with sand, insert gold, silver, or white candles into the center, and cover with glass hurricane globes to line your stairs or mantelpiece.

5. Decorate a small table tree with French ribbon bows (the wire rims hold their shape), then add silver balls and lots of tiny clear lights. Place the tree in a terra-cotta pot or in an oversized crock or container that can be wrapped with gold mesh, fabric, or pretty paper. Wrap small token gifts for everyone who visits during the holidays and place them around the tree.

6. Intimate sitdown dinners for six or eight have become increasingly popular. If your house is small or you can't manage a large party, consider a couple of small dinner parties.

HOLIDAY CRAFTING

People aren't filling their leisure time with make-work anymore, but they are making things related to home decorating. And never is it more evident than during the holidays. The stores are filled with materials for all sorts of crafting during this time of year, and even if you feel all thumbs most of the time, crafting for Christmas couldn't be easier.

A Survey of Most Popular Crafts

Reporting on a craft and hobby study, Pat Koziol, director of the Hobby Industries of America, reports that crafts have exploded in the 1990s. You might be interested to know what sorts of crafts are the most popular from a survey taken of three thousand people across the country. Hard crafts having to do with woodworking and furniture decorating are number one, with painting and drawing second. Needlecrafts fell from number one to three in the past few years, followed by sewing and floral crafts.

Nature Crafts

Making a natural wreath or centerpiece is the beginning of a holiday welcome. For all the fixings you could ever want, visit your home center and don't forget the things you can find outdoors like pine cones and branches. It's easy to add them to a plain straw wreath with a craft glue gun found in all five and dimes, hobby shops, and home centers.

Finding Materials

Mail order is one way to find materials. As with everything else we buy, shopping by mail for craft materials is easy. Aside from the many catalogs available, there are lots of small companies that specialize in things like miniature stencils, beads, flower arranging materials, sequins, ribbons, and more. Check out the many craft magazines that proliferate at this time of year and you'll find the names of advertisers for supplies at the back of the books.

Personalized Gifts

If someone you know was married this year or had a new baby, use the printed invitation or announcement to make a unique gift. Mount it to a painted wooden plaque or box top and surround it with appropriate cutout paper designs. These might come from wrapping paper, cards, or books. Apply several coats of varnish to protect the paper. I use water-base varnish for quick drying and have found I like it better than polyurethane.

Gifts from Scraps

Use buttons to decorate plain items like a heart-shaped lace sachet. Outline a heart of sewn-on buttons. Or use little white pearl buttons to glue around a plain frame. This is nice for a baby picture. Think of new ways to use scraps and you'll come up with all sorts of interesting gift ideas. My favorite is making a baby quilt from scrap fabrics. Choose all your pastel fabrics or make a patchwork from soft flannels.

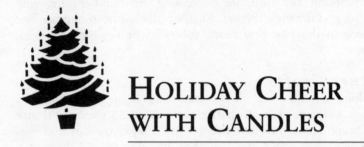

HOLIDAY CHEER WITH CANDLES

Cherubs, angels, holly, evergreens, pine cones, wreaths, garlands, gold, silver, red-and-green plaid, tinsel, stars, and cranberry strings are all the finishing touches of Christmas decorating. One of the most elegant, affordable, and easy ways to add a festive touch to every room is with candles.

The following thirteen tips are some of my favorites for adding holiday cheer with candles.

1. If you're entertaining during the holidays, burn candles in every room to create a total holiday ambience. Use cranberry-, evergreen-, peppermint-, and raspberry-scented candles to evoke a holiday scent throughout the house. Or, if you are using an all-white theme, use only white candles in different sizes. Don't forget those wonderful fat candles that come in different heights.
2. Metallic gold candles add a touch of elegance, whether burned on the mantel or at the dinner table. Use them in brass holders.
3. Keep wrapped votive candles and pretty votive holders on hand to use as gifts for drop-in holiday guests.

4. Candles make the difference between dining and just eating. Make a holiday centerpiece by filling a white bowl with evergreens, add pine cones here and there on the branches, and surround the bowl with candles in holders of different size and height.

5. Use decorative trims such as a candle ring of holly leaves and berries or gold poinsettias around the base of the candle to dress it up.

6. Have you seen the unglazed ceramic cherubs available in gift shops? Some of them are candle holders and they come in different sizes and positions. I'd give them a spray coat of pearl finish so they glow.

7. If you don't have lots of candle holders it's actually more interesting to use glass jars, wide-mouth heavy glasses, brandy snifters, and globe-like vases from the florist. Empty baby-food jars can be used to hold votive candles. Be creative and look for items to turn into candle holders for a grouping of different sizes and heights. I've even used old salt and pepper shakers turned upside down with the plastic stoppers removed for holding narrow candles.

8. Buy the long matches used for lighting a fire in the fireplace or one of those automatic lighters sold for the grill to reach into a hurricane lamp or deep vase.

9. For almost anyone on your list, a candle snuffer along with a box of white dripless candles is a nice holiday gift. I never feel secure without a full box of white candles in my cabinet. If you can find the ones imported from France with holes in the top for allowing the wax to drip back down inside the candle, they are sensational. I use mine very sparingly. I've been able to find them only now and then at Wolfman Gold and Good Company in New York City. If you find them, buy as many as you can.

10. Everyone looks better by candlelight. Even your furniture will look better. Entertain holiday guests in the flattering glow of candlelight by combining candles of various heights and widths in an elegant grouping on a coffee table, side table, mantle, or dining table.

11. If you have a table against a wall, fill a large glass bowl with a string of tiny clear Christmas tree bulbs and conceal the cord behind the table. Add lots of votives on either side of the

bowl. I especially like a pure white, lace-edged runner under it all.

12. Use small toys to create a playful scene. Then intersperse small red and green candles (the large size "birthday" candles are good for this) in chunky wooden holders for a whimsical display.

13. Make your own candle holders from blocks of wood. It's easy to drill a hole in the top of each, then spray-paint them in red, white, or green—or faux-finish them with marble and line them up on the mantle. If you're feeling creative, make enough to spell out a word like "CHEERS" or "NOEL'" and stencil one letter on the front of each block candleholder. Place them on a mantel covered with greens and add small shiny colorful tree balls and pine cones between the candles.

WREATHS

The wreath has long been a popular decoration for the holidays, positioned on doors and windows or accenting walls and mantelpieces. Wreaths have also grown in popularity as craft projects, with crafters customizing their Christmas decorations to reflect their own decor.

Hydrangea Wreath

Have you ever seen a dried hydrangea wreath? Many people make them for year-round display, not just during the holidays. Since hydrangeas come in several colors, some wreaths are made of faded blue, others from the wine-colored blossoms, and some from pale green. Picked while still fresh, they are pinned and wired to a straw wreath. As they dry out they retain their color, but become slightly brittle and are therefore meant only for indoor use. Some people do put them on the  front door, knowing they will look inviting for a while, even if they won't last forever. They are reminders of a fading summer, but can be enjoyed all year. Hang them inside your windows with a red or green satin or velvet ribbon and you'll have a classic holiday look for several months.

Crafting Tradition

According to the Hobby Industry Association, people are making more Christmas decorations for their own use first, and as gifts a close second. Wreath-making is extremely popular because you can achieve beautiful results using simple, readily available products such as ribbons and beads.

Personalized Wreath

One easy-to-make, yet totally unique wreath is made with personal mementos. Just collect small treasures from shelves and hidden-away boxes to display on your memory wreath. Use tiny framed photos, small ornaments, toys, teddy bears, bells, shells, starfish, tiny sachet bags, dried baby's breath and roses, little birds, pins, earrings, small wooden animals, Christmas stickers, charms, small china figures, berries, little baskets, and tiny wrapped boxes.

How to Do It

You will need the following:

a 30-inch artificial pine wreath

about sixty small mementos

twenty small bows, each made with different ribbon or strips of fabric like calico (if you have pinking shears use these to cut 1/2-inch-wide strips)

four yards of red-wired beads

a glue gun with glue sticks (or you can wire the ribbon and mementos to the wreath).

1. Glue your treasures to the wreath, arranging the colors and items evenly.
2. Tie ribbon scraps of all kinds into bows and glue the bows onto the wreath at random. Pieces of lace can be tied into small bows and added.
3. Wind the red-wired beads around the wreath. Tack beads to wreath with dots of glue.

ELEGANT DECORATING FOR THE HOLIDAYS

Low-key, understated tasteful, elegant, simple. These are the words to describe this year's approach to holiday decorating. In keeping with this idea I've already started making a few things for my house. This is a good time to make a vine wreath or select one of pine branches adorned with a simple ribbon. While the felt red bow is traditional, consider satin white or silver this year.

Pine Cones

Pine cones make a wonderful table decoration. I sprayed a bunch with an iridescent icicle pearl finish so they have a shimmery glow. Place them in a basket, add sprigs of holly, and set it on a hallway table. Or, if you want to do some minimal creative crafting, glue the pine cones to a wreath made of honeysuckle vines. A small glue gun works best for this sort of project.

Tree Balls

Start to make tree ornaments this weekend. Styrofoam balls come in small, medium, and large sizes. I used these balls as the basis for one of my holiday decoration projects. It takes seconds to give them the medieval look of stone balls. Spray them with Formby's faux granite finish that comes in an aerosol can.

You can spray the Styrofoam balls one of two ways. First insert straight pins up through a piece of cardboard. Press each ball onto the tip of a pin to hold it in place for spraying. Or, you can insert a length of wire into the ball and slowly turn it while spraying with the other hand. Either method works fine.

Once the balls are dry, they can be decorated with a very full plaid or satin taffeta bow on top, sprigs of artificial holly and berries, a bell, or other decorations. There are lots of dried materials in the garden shops for adding to your ornaments. Secure them with the hot glue gun. You can use Elmer's craft glue, but it takes longer to dry and isn't as strong. Make a hanging loop with a piece of 1/8-inch-wide ribbon and secure the raw ends with a pin stuck into the top of the Styrofoam. All of the materials for making these ornaments are available at home centers, craft shops, and fabric stores.

For Those Who Are All Thumbs

If you're of the "I'd rather buy it than make it" school, there are loads of exquisite ornaments around for all tastes and all pocketbooks. But before buying a little here and a little there, plan a theme. This is the year for everything to be of one piece. For example, it might be a romantic theme in which case all your ornaments might be lacy and old-fashioned and made of pastel colors. Frankly, I'm tired of the country theme, but the true red and green colors of Christmas are always attractive.

For the Tree

I like a tree with only small white lights and that's it. However, during the years that I lived in The Big Apple, I collected a whole bunch of shiny red apples in all sizes and can't bear not to cover the tree with them. Then there are the handmade ornaments Jon and my daughters and I designed and made over the years for the many Christmas books we produced. I take out the boxes and look at them longingly. But I'm determined to stick with a pure white theme, the one I always find most appealing.

For the Table

Add a bit of gold and silver in the form of candles and table trimmings for sparkle and you can't possibly fail to be perfectly in style.

For Tradition's Sake

Christmas isn't really about style. It's about tradition. So take solace. No matter how you decorate for Christmas it will always be just right, and if you do the same thing every year it will become a tradition. No matter what the trendsetters say, if you like what you've always done for years and years, don't mess with tradition. It's a style unto itself.

Ten Last-Minute Gift Wraps That Don't Look It!

Before Martha Stewart demonstrated how creatively one could wrap presents in just under five hours per gift and for less than $20 for each wrap (not including the cost for the faux finishing classes one needed before beginning), my brother-in-law was into unusual gift papers. One Christmas all his gifts were wrapped with a wide assortment of maps you get from gas stations. Another year brought collage wrappings made from an assortment of torn magazine pages.

I'm not too fond of colorful commercial wrapping paper, but I'm not fanatic enough to spend weeks making paper that will cause me to come unhinged when the recipients tear into my gifts. Once you've finished your shopping, it's fun to spread the gifts about and wrap them. Even if you haven't made one single present, it's easy to be a creative wrapper. This is the time to take out all the odds and ends of ribbons, sequins, fabric scraps, buttons, paint, stencils, and other craft materials. Put on some Christmas music, make cider or egg nog or a good cup of tea, and settle in for a day of wrapping.

The following are some of my favorite ideas:

1. Use brown Kraft paper as the base for a really classy wrap. Add gold marbleizing or sponge painting at random over the entire roll of paper for all your gifts. Or, cut a star stencil from a manila folder and use gold paint to fill in a random pattern of stars over the paper. Tie the package with wired, gold mesh ribbon.

2. If you're mailing packages, even at a late date, you won't want crushed bows. Large stencil letters are perfect for a holiday message or the person's name. Wrap each gift in shiny

red, green, white, gold, or silver paper. For an economical wrap, use white shiny shelf lining or butcher paper and stencil designs like holly, trees, and bows over all sides. The stenciled bow on top replaces a fabric bow.

3. With pinking sheers, cut up scraps of pretty fabrics like velvet, moire, taffeta, and satin and glue them in a crazy-quilt pattern to a plain box. Add buttons, sequins, rickrack, and bits of lace or ribbon here and there. Tie with rickrack or a 2-inch-wide strip of fabric cut with pinking sheers.

4. Give gifts in plain brown paper bags. Draw a large circle on the front of the bag to form the "base" of a wreath. Then use a rubber stamp with a Christmas image, such as pine branches or holly leaves, and green ink to stamp a wreath design around the circle. (If you can't find a green ink pad, use Magic Marker on the stamp.) Tie a ribbon in pretty loops to make a fancy bow. Glue a real sprig of greens or a bell to the wreath on the front of the bag. Fill the bag with lots of red or green tissue to surround your gift.

5. Wrap your gifts in Kraft paper. Collect a handful of leaves and spray-paint them gold. Arrange the leaves and glue them to the paper. Coat three pine cones with the gold paint and glue to the top of the box. You can also do this with acorns.

6. Sheets of newspaper make a terrific-looking wrapping paper. After the gift is wrapped, coat it with shiny quick-drying water-base varnish. Tie each package with a red plaid taffeta bow.

7. If you have old sheet music, use it to wrap up a gift for a music lover.

8. For an intimate gift like perfume or lingerie, wrap the box in pure white. Attach a doily to the top and write your message. Tie with a piece of eyelet, lace, or white satin ribbon. Tuck a dried rosebud into the knot of the bow.

9. If you're out of paper and it's too late to buy more, use all your scraps to make a patchwork quilt pattern. Cut up squares and triangles of wrapping paper or magazine pages as you would with fabric, and glue them to the box top. Tie with yarn, string, ribbon, or embroidery thread.

10. If you're like me, you have lots of family snapshots that never got into the album. Use them to create a gift wrap for your children to give to their grandparents. Center a child's photo

on a piece of plain paper large enough to go around the gift. Then surround the edges of the photo with a frame made from ribbons, buttons, sequins, or whatever you have on hand.

CHRISTMAS AT HOME

The thought of snow for Christmas is a Northern fantasy. It's a symbol of pureness that blankets the scenery. White and crystal clear represent a nice theme for holiday decorating as well as for gifts for the home. When you have a theme to work around, it makes shopping a little easier.

Here are some ideas for pure and simple Christmas gifts and decorations:

1. Give everyone thick white bath towels. Don't box them, but rather swathe them in lots of white tissue paper and tie with beautiful white- or gold-wire-rimmed ribbon in a lavish bow. Make gift tags from small lacy doilies and write names with a gold tip pen. Add a wooden-handled scrub brush or bath salts under each bow.

2. A live tree in a huge terra-cotta pot is ecological, and it can be planted after the holidays. I like a small (about 4 foot), perfectly shaped tree placed in an interesting pot filled with sand to hold it in place. Cover the tree with clear lights and silver balls for a most elegant decoration.

3. Use clear round glass votive candle holders and group them everywhere. Always use white candles.

4. Take away all accessories from all tabletops and start over from scratch. Only use white or natural-colored items such as twig baskets filled with pine cones.

5. Using a glue gun and Styrofoam balls, attach layers of bay leaves to cover the balls. Pile them into a terra-cotta dish.

6. Topiary trees in little clay pots are elegant when lined down the middle of a table. Place a lace-edged runner down first, then arrange the pots on top. Use pure white plates and deep-green linen napkins tied with white satin ribbons. Or use white linen napkins with gold napkin rings.

7. A single white orchid on a side table is all that's needed for freshness. Add a gold-rimmed white plate full of Christmas cookies for everyone to help themselves.

8. Fill ornate urns with sprawling ivy and place on either side of the mantel. Use three hurricane lamps with fat white candles inside between the urns.

9. Set the table with all white and silver. Polish everything you own. This is the time to use all those wedding gifts. Silver candlesticks look elegant with white beeswax candles; sterling dishes can be used to hold food, and sterling silverware instantly transforms any ordinary table or dishware. If you don't have enough silver, mix in a little pewter—for example, a small bowl to hold cranberries.

10. Fill an oversized basket with white poinsettias. Add green ivy tendrils to spill over the sides of the basket and top with Spanish moss around the plants.

11. Fill glass fruit compotes with gold balls in all sizes. Or use glass cake stands. Arrange the balls so you have a few very large ones on the bottom and lots of small balls piled around to look like golden cherries.

12. Dress up dining chairs by tying fat gold mesh bows to the chair backs.

13. Serve food that is selected for color as well as taste. And choose the serving dishes in the same way. If you don't have the right dish, wrap it with silver foil or shiny gift paper and add a gold cord around the outside rim.

14. Arrange pure white shells on a table or in a white bowl. Add sprigs of green. If you have a large enough shell, such as a big clam shell or conch shell, use it to hold a votive candle.

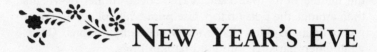

NEW YEAR'S EVE

New Year's Eve is my favorite of all the special times we celebrate. We always stay home alone and plan the evening exactly the way we like—our favorite food, candlelight, a fire in the fireplace, music that suits our particular mood, and a couple of good movies in case we actually stay up past eleven. It may not sound exciting, but it's just about the perfect setting for the onset of new beginnings. And that's what a new year represents.

Whatever you did right or wrong last year can be repeated or eliminated next year, and New Year's Eve is just a reminder of that fact. Some of us stick to resolutions, others just like the process of making them, saying them out loud, and then forgetting about them altogether. I admit, I fall into both categories. But I love the idea of fresh starts—the beginning of writing or reading a new book, the renewal of magazine subscriptions, the promise one more time to make those slipcovers for which I bought fabric two years ago, the resolve to keep a balanced checkbook, that old and tired resolve to lose 10 pounds, and on and on. As I get older the list actually gets shorter. I'm learning to set realistically low goals to ensure success.

Cozy Up

If, like us, you're cozying up for New Year's, plan ahead just as if you were throwing a dinner party. Make your home feel special. Low lights, a pretty table setting, a great meal, wonderful dessert for later, superb wine or champagne, just the right music, flowers, and whatever else it takes to make you feel like a guest at your own party. Depending on the ages of your children, work it out so they have an early celebration before going to bed.

Last-Minute Ideas for a New Year's Party

If you're having a few people in to help celebrate, here are some quick-and-easy tabletop decorations that don't take much money or time.

1. Cover the table or buffet with silver, gold, or white wrapping paper. You may have a seam down the center. Tape the paper along the seam and cover it with greens such as pine needles. Arrange pine cones on the greens and add gold or silver Christmas balls here and there for sparkle.

2. Buy ice cream sundae, glass dessert dishes (available at supermarkets) and place a votive candle in each. Then wrap with a tinsel garland or wired silver stars around the base and up the glass. For added effect, rim the top of the scalloped edge of the dessert glasses with sparkle glue. Arrange among the greenery.

3. Here are two different centerpiece ideas. The first is for those who are really all thumbs, don't have any time left, and can't be bothered with creativity. Simply fill a cut glass bowl with silver balls or lots of tinsel. It sparkles! For more impact, add a handful of clear tiny lights (a tangled string is perfect and you avoid the frustration of untangling). The second idea came to me while looking for ideas in the supermarket. It can also be used as a hostess gift. Wrap a plastic plant holder with brown Kraft paper (or use white, gold, or silver). Tuck the paper edges into the top of the planter. Tie a gold cord or raffia wrap around the rim. Fill the bottom half of the planter with scrunched-up newspaper or tissue. On top of this you will place a very full head of red or green cabbage or kale, but first scoop out the center large enough to hold three or four beautiful red pears. Fan out the leaves over the top of the bucket and arrange the pears on top. Place a sprig of holly or a pine cone on top or on the side of the pears or add a variety of nuts to fill in the spaces.

A designer friend, artfully, and I might add sparingly, places pears along her mantelpiece. No greens, no lights, just the pears. And they look spectacular!

4. For a buffet it's always best to have oversized napkins, which I call "lapnaps." You can make as many as you need in minutes. With a pencil, draw 22- or 24-inch squares on the back of colorful fabric. All the napkins can be different so use up your scrap fabric. Since most fabric is 45 inches wide, you'll get two from a width. Use pinking shears to cut out each square. No sewing involved. Fold the square on the diagonal to make a

large triangle. Place your silverware setting with the handles on the point of the fabric. Fold each corner in and roll the fabric so it's narrow at the bottom and the cut edges fan out on the top. Tie with ribbons and insert a bit of greenery.

These little finishing touches will make the table festive and add to the anticipation of a bright and promising New Year. Have a Happy!

Index